ITALIAN

for travellers

CONVERSATION HANDBOOK

4000 words • 2000 phrases

GIUNTI

project
Paolo Piazzesi

editing
Aldo Castellani
Christiane Splinter

translation
Michael Barbour
Colleen Campbell
Stephanie Johnson

phonetics
Leonardo Lavacchi

graphic design
Matteo Lucii

impagination
Stefania Cinotti

The Situation on coeliac disease (pages 106-107) has been written and translated by Aldo Castellani.

www.giunti.it

© 1999, 2007 Giunti Editore S.p.A.
Via Bolognese, 165 - 50139 Firenze - Italia
Via Dante, 4 - 20121 Milano - Italia
Prima edizione: 1999
Nuova edizione: gennaio 2007

Ristampa	Anno
6 5 4 3	2013 2012 2011 2010

Stampato presso Giunti Industrie Grafiche S.p.A. Stabilimento di Prato

This newly conceived phrase book contains nearly 4000 terms and over 2000 phrases, organised into 5 Areas (Understanding, Travelling, Living, Problem Solving, Discovering) that are divided into various Situations. Each of these corresponds to real-life situations and to those basic and special needs that may arise during travels and stays in Italy. The phrases are listed following the order in which they would be stated in a real dialogue. A comprehensive range of phrases and terms is concentrated into the Situation in which they would be required. The Situations are also complete with possible or likely replies on behalf of an eventual Italian interlocutor.

We have given great space and importance to the indications for correctly pronouncing Italian terms and making oneself understood immediately. To identify each Situation within this phrase book, use the highly detailed Contents (next page); to immediately find a required word or transform the phrase book into a handy dictionary, simply consult the Rapid Index (page 191).

■ **HOW TO READ THE PHRASE BOOK**
- **bold face**, words and phrases in English;
- normal type, the relative translations;
- in the vocabulary of each Situation, in the third column, the transcription in IPA; instructions for pronouncing IPA signs and the phonetic transcription are found in "Basic Rules of Pronunciation";
- *cursive bold face* (in colour), questions and answers of your Italian interlocutors or texts from signs and loud speaker announcements;
- normal type, translations of these phrases, signs or announcements.

■ **DON'T FORGET...**
Some phrases leave space for various alternatives; these are marked by ellipses: the choice of the proper solution can be taken from the relative vocabulary or from the words listed in Area 1 (see further).
The phrase book is also a *source for communication* with the interlocutor. When in difficulty, in fact, you may simply show the page, **indicating the word or phrase that you wish to communicate** (you will find the "magic words" on page 191); you may also ask your interlocutor to do the same to indicate his reply or to answer your query.

CONTENTS

This detailed table of CONTENTS is an infallible **guide** to direct you through the Areas and Situations in order to immediately identify the pages where you will find the terms you require. Complementary to the contents, the **RAPID INDEX** (page 255) works as a **shortcut** to immediately locate the word or phase you need in any given moment and is a key for using the phrase book as a dictionary. Do you want to know how to say "Good night" in Italian? Look in the Rapid Index under "greetings" and in the vocabulary of page 23 you will find that you say "Buona notte". Don't forget to look among the "Useful words for Travelling" (Area 1.4) where you will surely find the noun, adjective, verb and adverb you need and which permit you to complete the open option phrases (*marked with ellipses*) and compose new phrases of your own.

BASIC RULES OF PRONUNCIATION 8

GRAMMAR TIPS 13

AREA 1 – *UNDERSTANDING* **15**

1.1 MEASURING TIME 16
Common expressions of time 16 – Time (hours and minutes) 17 – When (day and date) 18 – Days of the week 19 – Months 19 – The Seasons 19 – Holidays 20 – Temporal adverbs and expressions 20
1.2 THE WEATHER 21
1.3 DAILY VOCABULARY 23
Expressions of courtesy 23 – Interrogatives 23 – Greetings and salutations 24 – Expressions of approval and compliments 25 – Expressions of disapproval 25 – Personal pronouns (Subject and Object) 26 – Possessive adjectives and pronouns 26
1.4 USEFUL WORDS FOR TRAVELLING 27
One hundred important nouns 27 – Useful Adjectives and adverbs and their opposites 29 – The most common verbs 31 – Verb expressions 34 – Directions and locations 34
1.5 PHRASES YOU'LL SEE ON SIGNS 36
1.6 NUMBERS, WEIGHTS AND MEASURES 38
Cardinal numbers 38 – Ordinal numbers 40 – Weights and measures 41 – Temperature 42
1.7 COLOURS AND HUES 43

1.8 SPECIAL NEEDS 44
Smoking (and Non-smoking) 44 – The disabled 44 – Children 44 – Travelling with pets 45

AREA 2 – *TRAVELLING* 47

2.1 ON THE PLANE AND IN THE AIRPORT 48
In the Airport: check-in and boarding 48 – Common signs in airports 48 – Announcements you may hear on the loudspeaker 49 – **On the plane** 50 – Signs you may see and announcements you may hear on the plane 50 – **Arriving at destination** 51 – Customs 51 – **Leaving the airport** 52

2.2 IN THE CAR (OR ON A MOTORCYCLE) 53
Personal and car documents 53 – Signs you may see at country borders and toll booths 53 – Possible requests at customs 53 – Vehicles 54 – Various categories of roads and traffic 54 – **Directions in car travel** 55 – **Road signs** 55 – **At the service station** 57 – Refuelling and minor repairs 57 – The service station attendant or mechanic might say… 58 – **Parking** 59 – Traffic violations 60

2.3 ON THE FERRYBOAT, SHIP, HYDROPLANE 62
At the port and on board 62 – At the port 62 – At the ticket office 62 – On board 64

2.4 ON THE TRAIN 66
At the train station 66 – Information, tickets and reservations 66 – Announcements you may hear over the loudspeaker 69 – **On the train** 69

2.5 USING PUBLIC TRANSPORT 71
Taxis 71 – **Taking the bus, trolley or tram** 72 – On the bus 74 – **The underground** 74 – Signs you may see in the underground 75 – **Travelling on buses and coaches** 75 – On the coach 76

2.6 DOCUMENTS AND PUBLIC OFFICES 77

2.7 HIRING A CAR AND OTHER VEHICLES 78
Hiring a Car 78 – Hiring other means of transport 81

AREA 3 – *LIVING* 83

3.1 HOTELS 84
Hotel reservations 84 – Reserving through the local tourism bureau 85 – Reserving by phone or at the reception desk 87 – **When you get to**

your hotel 88 – Room service 89 – **During your stay** 91 – Problems with room or service 91 – Problems on the part of the hotel 93 – **Reserving a bed and breakfast hotel** 94 – Camping and holiday resorts 94 – **Reserving in youth hostels** 96 – **Apartments and boarding houses** 96 – **Checking out: Checking and paying your bill** 98

3.2 FOOD AND RESTAURANTS 99
Meals 99 – **Breakfast** 99 – **Choosing a restaurant** 101 – **Reserving a table** 102 – **At your table** 103 – **Placing your order** 104 – **For those who suffer from coeliac disease** 106 – **Cooking** 108 – Special diet request 109 – **Sauces, breads and condiments** 110 – **Drinks** 110 – **Full meals** 113 – Aperitifs and starters 113 – Salads 115 – First courses (soups and pasta dishes) 116 – Side dishes and herbs 117 – Second courses 119 – Fish 121 – Omelettes, pies and pizza 122 – Cheese 123 – Fruit 123 – Dessert 124 – Liqueurs and coffee 125 – **Snacks** 126 – **Changing your order, compliments and complaints** 127 – **Checking and paying the bill** 129

3.3 MONEY, POST OFFICES AND TELEPHONES 130
Asking prices and paying 130 – **Banks and currency exchange** 131 – **The post** 132 – **Public telephones** 133 – Sending a fax 136

3.4 BEAUTY AND HYGIENE 137
Personal hygiene 137 – Health and hygiene of newborns 137 – **Cosmetics and beauty** 138 – **The hairdresser, the barber** 140

3.5 RELIGION 142

AREA 4 – *PROBLEM SOLVING* **143**

4.1 EMERGENCIES 144
Danger and calamities 144 – Danger signs 146 – **Vehicle breakdown and repair** 147 – Car parts 147 – Mechanics and electrical system 148 – Interiors and commands 150 – **The mechanic's diagnosis** 153 – **Road accidents** 155 – **Missing persons** 158

4.2 THEFT, DAMAGE, ASSAULT 159
Theft and muggings 159 – **Damages** 161 – **Aggressions and assaults** 162

4.3 BEARINGS 163
Finding your bearings in the city 163

4.4 HEALTH 165
Illness and symptoms 165 – **Contagious diseases and viral infections** 167 – **Trauma** 168 – **Parts of the body** 168 – **Asking for medical**

assistance 171 – **Speaking with a doctor** 172 – Medical specialists 176 – **Anxiety and similar states** 177 – **The dentist, the orthodontist** 178 – **The optometrist** 180 – **Medical bills and payment** 180 – **The emergency room** 181 – Phrases useful during the ambulance ride and in the emergency room of a hospital 181 – **At the chemist's** 185

AREA 5 – *DISCOVERING* **189**

5.1 MEETING PEOPLE 190
The first approach 190 – **Information and advice** 191 – **Greetings and introductions** 192 – **Acquaintances and invitations** 192
5.2 SIGHTSEEING AND TOURS 194
Seeing the sights 194 – **Visiting museums, exhibits and collections** 196 – **Styles, techniques, objects and materials** 198 – **Churches and places of worship** 200 – **Tours, excursions and side trips** 202 – Cancellations and complaints 203 – **At the seaside, the lake, the river** 203 – **Outdoors** 205 – Signs you may see during your excursion 206
5.3 ENTERTAINMENT AND LEISURE 207
Cinema, theatre, concerts 207 – Programs and tickets 207 – Signs you may see or announcements you may hear at the theatre 208 – Information on shows 210 – Inside the theatre 210 – **Night clubs and discotheques** 211 – Dressing appropriately 211 – **Sports and sporting events** 212 – Main athletic disciplines 213 – Other sports 214 – Winter sports 217 – Signs you may see on the ski-runs 217 – **Cards and games** 218
5.4 SHOPPING 221
Looking for a shop, an object, a service 221 – **In the shop** 223 – Watch for signs that say… 223 – **Department stores, supermarkets and shopping centres** 225 – Fabrics 225 – **Clothing** 227 – **Sewing items** 229 – **Undergarments** 229 – **Hats, ties and accessories** 229 – **Leather goods and baggage** 230 – **Shoes and shoe repair** 230 – **Food stuffs** 233 – **Household items** 236 – **Electricity and electrical appliances** 238 – **Music, stereo and Hi-Fi** 239 – **The bookshop, the news-stand** 240 – **Stationers and art supplies** 241 – **Laundry and dry cleaners** 243 – **Jewellers** 244 – **Photography** 247 – **The Optician** 249 – **The Tobacco shop** 250 – **Local handicrafts Products** 251 – **The Florist** 252 – **Making the decision, negotiating, paying** 253 – The negative decision 253 – The positive decision 254

HANDY REFERENCE GUIDE 255

BASIC RULES OF PRONUNCIATION

When speaking their own language, Italians rarely succeed in avoiding those prosodic or articulating features that are typical of their region of origin. There is, nevertheless, an ideal pronunciation of Italian which is taught in acting schools and which can be defined as Florentine purified of some of its idiomatic characteristics. The phonetic transcription of the words in this phrase book is based upon this ideal pronunciation and it is proper that a foreigner should aspire to speak it as such.

The greatest difficulties that foreigners, as well as some Italians, encounter lie in the pronunciation of those sounds that are not represented univocally in writing and in the stress, which only appears when it falls on the last syllable.

We believe that these difficulties are, however, easily overcome if one follows the phonetic transcription presented here closely; it has been modelled after, with some simplifications, the International Phonetic Alphabet. We present below the sounds that comprise the Italian language, with examples of English words in which the sounds are found.

■ SOUNDS THAT ARE NOT PRESENT IN THE ENGLISH LANGUAGE

The English speakers who use this manual should give particular attention to those sounds which are not present in their own language, for which a brief explanation is necessary:

– [ts] (unvoiced dental affricative) with the voiced correspondent [dz]. The resonance which derives from the vibration of the vocal cords is absent in unvoiced consonants; for example in *duty* the *t* is unvoiced and the *d* is voiced. The sound [ts] can be obtained by pronouncing the two consonants of the symbol one following the other to create the sound like that of the two *zs* in the Italian word *pizza*.

– [ʎ] (lateral palatal fricative) In Italian it is always double as in the word *figli*. It is similar to the sound of the two *ls* in the word *million*, pronounced with greater intensity.

– [ɲ] (lateral nasal fricative) This sound differs from the above mainly for its nasality. Hence rather than the two *ls* of *million*,

8

it is comprised of two *ns*. This is the sound of the group *gn* in the Italian word *gnocchi* or in the French word *cognac*.

The Italian language also holds double consonants which are pronounced with a greater stress and intensity.

The stress symbol is ['] and precedes the stressed syllable. The stress falls therefore on the first vowel after the symbol. Remember that the symbols [j] and [w] are not vowels but semiconsonants and are therefore never stressed.

■ VOWELS

graph. repr.	phon. repr.	italian example	pronun.	tips for pronunciation
a	[a]	**c**asa	'kasa	like the *a* in *large*.
e	[e]	p**e**ra	'pera	like the *e* in *men*.
e	[ɛ]	**e**cco	'ɛkko	like the *e* in *extra*.
i	[i]	**i**nverno	in'vɛrno	like the *i* in *pin*.
o	[o]	**o**ra	'ora	like the *o* in *open*.
o	[ɔ]	r**o**sa	'rɔza	like the couple *aw* in *paw*.
u	[u]	**u**no	'uno	like the couple *oo* in *book*.

■ SEMICONSONANTS

graph. repr.	phon. repr.	italian example	pronun.	tips for pronunciation
i	[j]	**i**eri	'jɛri	like the *y* in *year*.
u	[u]	**u**omo	'wɔmo	like the *w* in *wonderful*.

■ CONSONANTS

graph. repr.	phon. repr.	italian example	pronun.	tips for pronunciation
b	[b]	**b**ello	'bɛllo	like the *b* in *box*.
		ne**bb**ia	'nebbja	
c	[k]	**c**asa	'kasa	before *a, o, u*, like
		ri**cc**o	'rikko	the *c* in *cold*.

9

graph. repr.	phon. repr.	italian example	pronun.	tips for pronunciation
c	[tʃ]	**c**ena	'tʃena	before *i*, *e*, like the *ch* in *cheese*.
		ro**cce**	'rɔttʃe	
ch	[k]	**ch**iave	'kjave	before *i*, *e* like the *k* in *kitchen*.
		ve**cch**io	'vekkjo	
ci	[tʃ]	**ci**ao	'tʃao	before *a*, *e*, *o*, *u*, like the couple *ch* in *change*.
		ca**cci**a	'kattʃa	
		farma**cia**	farma'tʃia	when the *i* is stressed, it should be pronounced.
d	[d]	**d**ente	'dɛnte	like the *d* in *dog*.
		a**dd**io	ad'dio	
f	[f]	**f**umo	'fumo	like the *f* in *fish*.
		ca**ff**è	kaf'fɛ	
g	[g]	**g**ara	'gara	before *a*, *o*, *u*, like the *g* in *gold*.
		le**gg**o	'lɛggo	
g	[dʒ]	**g**iro	'dʒiro	before *i*, *e*, like the *g* in *general*.
		le**gg**e	'leddʒɛ	
gh	[g]	**gh**iro	'giro	before *i*, *e* like the couple *gu* in *guest*.
		a**ggh**indare	aggin'dare	
gi	[dʒ]	**gi**orno	'dʒorno	before *a*, *e*, *o*, *u* like the couple *dg* in *bridge*.
		pe**ggi**ore	ped'dʒore	
		ener**gia**	ener'dʒia	when the *i* is stressed, it should be pronounced.
gl	[ʎ]	fi**gl**i	'fiʎʎi	before *i*. See the section on sounds not present in English.
gli	[ʎ]	a**gli**o	'aʎʎo	before *a*, *e*, *o*, *u*. See the section on sounds not present in English.
gn	[ɲ]	ba**gn**o	'baɲɲo	See the section on sounds not present in English.

graph. repr.	phon. repr.	italian example	pronun.	tips for pronunciation
gu	[gw]	**gu**erra	'gwɛrra	before vowel; like the couple *gu* in *penguin*.
h		**h**anno	'anno	Silent; after *c, g*; see above.
l	[l]	pa**l**a pa**ll**a	'pala 'palla	like the *l* in *look*.
m	[m]	**m**useo go**mm**a	mu'zɛo 'gomma	like the *m* in *man*.
n	[n]	**n**otte pa**nn**a	'nɔtte 'panna	like the *n* in *night*.
p	[p]	**p**ane do**pp**io	'pane 'doppjo	like the *p* in *cap*.
qu	[kw]	**qu**ando	'kwando	like the group *qu* in *quiet*.
cqu	[kkw]	a**cqu**a	ak'kwa	As in the preceding example, but double.
r	[r]	**r**uota ca**rr**o	'rwɔta 'karro	like the *r* in *room*, but rolled/trilled, like *r* in Spanish or Scottish.
s	[s]	**s**era ro**ss**o	'sera 'rosso	like the *s* in *sit*.
s	[z]	ro**s**a	'rɔza	like the *s* in *these*, but never double.
sc	[ʃ]	u**sc**ita	uʃ'ʃita	before *i, e* like the group *sh* in *she*, always double.
sci	[ʃ]	la**sci**are	laʃ'ʃare	before *a, o, u*, like the group *sh* in *shop*, always double.
t	[t]	**t**oro pe**tt**o	'tɔro 'pɛtto	like the *t* in *table*.
v	[v]	**v**uoto o**vv**io	'vwɔto 'ɔvvjo	like the *v* in *very*.

graph. repr.	phon. repr.	italian example	pronun.	tips for pronunciation
z	[ts]	polizia piazza	polit'tsia 'pjattsa	See the section on sounds not present in English, always doubled.
z	[dz]	zoo razzo	'dzɔɔ 'raddzo	See the section on sounds not present in English, always doubled.

Here is the Italian alphabet, and beside it the names of the letters and their pronunciations.

a	a	a
b	bi	bi
c	ci	tʃi
d	di	di
e	e	e
f	effe	'ɛffe
g	gi	dʒi
h	acca	'akka
i	i	i
l	elle	'ɛlle
m	emme	'ɛmme
n	enne	'ɛnne
o	o	ɔ
p	pi	pi
q	cu	ku
r	erre	'ɛrre
s	esse	'ɛsse
t	ti	ti
u	u	u
v	vu	vu
z	zeta	'dzɛta

There are five other letters used in Italian but which are found only in words of foreign origin:

j	i lunga	il ' lunga
k	cappa	' kappa
w	vu doppia	vud ' doppja
x	ics	iks
y	ipsilon (i greca)	' ipsilon (ig ' grɛka)

The verbs *to be* and *to have* are auxiliary verbs also in Italian. Their infinitives are, respectively, *essere* and *avere*. Here is the conjugation of the Present Tense of both verbs:

Essere

Io (*I*)	sono (*am*)	' io ' sono
Tu (*you*)	sei (*are*)	tu ' sei
Egli, ella,		' eλλi ' ella
lui, lei (*he, she, it*)	è (*is*)	' lui, ' lɛi ɛ
Noi (*we*)	siamo (*are*)	' noi ' siamo
Voi (*you*)	siete (*are*)	' voi ' sjɛte
Essi, loro (*they*)	sono (*are*)	' loro ' sono

Avere

Io (*I*)	ho (*have*)	' io ɔ
Tu (*you*)	hai (*have*)	tu ai
Egli, ella,		' eλλi ' ella
lui, lei (*he, she, it*)	ha (*has*)	' lui, ' lɛi a
Noi (*we*)	abbiamo (*have*)	' noi ab ' bjamo
Voi (*you*)	avete (*have*)	' voi a ' vete
Essi, loro (*they*)	hanno (*have*)	' loro ' anno

The personal pronouns are seldom used in Italian, hence our writing them in brackets. The preferred courtesy form used to address a person is *Lei* (written with capital letter) plus the third person singular of the verb. *Voi* as a courtesy form (plus the second person plural of the verb) is still in common use only in southern Italy. Thus, if you hear f.i. the phrase *lei è*, it may mean, according to the context, both *she is* and *you are* (courtesy form). Regular verbs follow in Italian three conjugation patterns, according to their infinitive ending in *–are*, *–ere*, or *–ire*. Here are some examples of the three patterns at the Present Tense:

Lavorare [*lavo'rare*] to work

Io (*I*)	lavoro (*work*)	*'io la'voro*
Tu (*you*)	lavori (*work*)	*tu la'vori*
Egli, ella,		*'eλλi'ella*
lui, lei (*he, she, it*)	lavora (*works*)	*'lui, 'lɛi la'vora*
Noi (*we*)	lavoriamo (*work*)	*'noi lavo'rjamo*
Voi (*you*)	lavorate (*work*)	*'voi lavo'rate*
Essi, loro (*they*)	lavorano (*work*)	*'loro la'vorano*

Prendere [*'prendere*] to take

Io (*I*)	prendo (*take*)	*'io 'prɛndo*
Tu (*you*)	prendi (*take*)	*tu 'prɛndi*
Egli, ella,		*'eλλi'ella*
lui, lei (*he, she, it*)	prende (*takes*)	*'lui, 'lɛi 'prɛnde*
Noi (*we*)	prendiamo (*take*)	*'noi prɛn'diamo*
Voi (*you*)	prendete (*take*)	*'voi prɛn'dete*
Essi, loro (*they*)	prendono (*take*)	*'loro 'prɛndono*

Partire [*par'tire*] to leave

Io (*I*)	parto (*leave*)	*'io 'parto*
Tu (*you*)	parti (*leave*)	*tu 'parti*
Egli, ella,		*'eλλi'ella*
lui, lei (*he, she, it*)	parte (*leaves*)	*'lui, 'lɛi 'parte*
Noi (*we*)	partiamo (*leave*)	*'noi par'tjamo*
Voi (*you*)	partite (*leave*)	*'voi par'tite*
Essi, loro (*they*)	partono (*leave*)	*'loro 'partono*

Intonation is a significant feature in Italian prosody. Thanks to intonation it is possible to convey an interrogation without changing the structure of the sentence. Example:

Antonio è italiano. **Antonio is Italian.**
Antonio è italiano? (*rising intonation*) **Is Antonio Italian?**

AREA 1. UNDERSTANDING

I n this Area, which concentrates more on words than on phrases, you will find the words and common expressions which comprise the basic vocabulary necessary in all countries to understand, be understood and to communicate in any moment. **It is important to understand that this section completes and supplements the following sections**: for example, if you would like to know how to pronounce a number, a requirement for making a phone call or paying a bill, you will find the answer here (in the phrases of the following Areas, in fact, you will find ellipses in place of numbers, indicating the necessity of completing the phrase of your own accord); should you wish to learn the names of the days, to reserve a hotel room or a table, or how to ask and say the time, you will have to consult this section; should you wish to memorise the common expressions of courtesy that are necessary to make any sort of query, you will need to study this Area. By the way, a word of advice: it is difficult (if not impossible) to obtain anything without pronouncing the magic words: **per favore**.

1.1
MEASURING TIME

1.2
THE WEATHER

1.3
DAILY VOCABULARY

1.4
USEFUL WORDS FOR TRAVELLING

1.5
PHRASES YOU'LL SEE ON SIGNS

1.6
NUMBERS, WEIGHTS AND MEASURES

1.7
COLOURS AND HUES

1.8
SPECIAL NEEDS

1.1 MEASURING TIME

time	tempo	'tɛmpo
dawn	alba	'alba
sunrise	aurora	au'rɔra
morning	mattino	mat'tino
midnight	mezzanotte	meddza'nɔtte
midday	mezzogiorno	meddzo'dʒorno
night	notte	'nɔtte
afternoon	pomeriggio	pome'riddʒo
evening	sera	'sera
sunset	tramonto	tra'monto
year	anno	'anno
date	data	'data
equinox	equinozio	ekwi'nɔttsjo
day	giorno	'dʒorno
month	mese	'mese
minute	minuto	mi'nuto
hour	ora	'ora
century	secolo	'sɛkolo
second	secondo	se'kondo
week	settimana	setti'mana
season	stagione	sta'dʒone

■ COMMON EXPRESSIONS OF TIME

by the end of the month	entro il mese	'entro il'mese
every other day	a giorni alterni	ad'dʒorni al'tɛrni
in the evening	in serata	inse'rata
in the morning	in mattinata	inmatti'nata
last month	il mese scorso	il'mese 'skorso
next month	il mese prossimo	il'mese 'prɔssimo
once a week	una volta alla settimana	una'vɔlta allasetti'mana
the day after	dopodomani	dopodo'mani
this evening	stasera	sta'sera
this morning	stamattina	stamat'tina

this week	questa settimana	'kwesta setti'mana
this year	quest'anno	kwes'tanno
today	oggi	'ɔddʒi
tomorrow	domani	do'mani
tomorrow evening	domani sera	do'mani 'sera
tomorrow morning	domattina	domat'tina
tonight	stanotte	sta'nɔtte
two days ago	due giorni fa	'due 'dʒorni fa
yesterday	ieri	'jɛri

■ TIME (HOURS AND MINUTES)

What is the time?
Che ore sono?
ke'ore 'sɔno

It...
Sono ...
'sɔno

... is three o'clock (exactly).	... le tre (in punto).	le'tre im'punto
... is five past three.	... le tre e cinque.	le'tre et'tʃinkwe
... is ten past three.	... le tre e dieci.	le'tre ed'djɛtʃi
... is a quarter past three.	... le tre e un quarto.	le'tre eun'kwarto
... is twenty-five past three.	... le tre e venticinque.	le'tre evventi'tʃinkwe
... is half past three.	... le tre e mezza.	le'tre em'mɛddza
... is twenty to four.	... le quattro meno venti.	le'kwattro meno'venti
... is a quarter to four.	... le quattro meno un quarto.	le'kwattro menoun'kwarto

It's midday/midnight.
È mezzogiorno/mezzanotte.

1.1 MEASURING TIME

At what time?
A che ora?
At half past seven in the morning.
Alle sette e mezza di mattina.
At a quarter past nine in the evening.
Alle nove e un quarto di sera.
From nine am to three pm.
Dalle nove alle tre. [9.00 - 15.00]

■ WHEN (DAY AND DATE)

Until when?
Fino a quando?
Until tomorrow.
Fino a domani.
What day is it today?
Che giorno è oggi?
Today is Saturday. It's the twenty-third of June 2007.
Oggi è sabato. È il ventitré giugno duemilasette.
Every Tuesday.
Ogni martedì.
In which month?
In che mese?
In August.
In agosto.
For how long?
Per quanto tempo?
How often?
Con che frequenza?
How long ago?
Quanto tempo fa?
Five days ago.
Cinque giorni fa.
In five days' time.
Fra cinque giorni.

DAYS OF THE WEEK

Monday	lunedì	lune'di
Tuesday	martedì	marte'di
Wednesday	mercoledì	merkole'di
Thursday	giovedì	dʒove'di
Friday	venerdì	vener'di
Saturday	sabato	'sabato
Sunday	domenica	do'menika

MONTHS

January	gennaio	dʒen'najo
February	febbraio	feb'brajo
March	marzo	'martso
April	aprile	a'prile
May	maggio	'maddʒo
June	giugno	'dʒuɲɲo
July	luglio	'luʎʎo
August	agosto	a'gosto
September	settembre	set'tɛmbre
October	ottobre	ot'tobre
November	novembre	no'vɛmbre
December	dicembre	di'tʃembre
high season	alta stagione	'alta sta'dʒone
low season	bassa stagione	'bassa sta'dʒone

THE SEASONS

Winter	inverno	in'vɛrno
Spring	primavera	prima'vera
Summer	estate	es'tate
Autumn	autunno	au'tunno

HOLIDAYS

New Year's Day	Capodanno	kapo'danno
Epiphany	Epifania	epifa'nia
Carnival	Carnevale	karne'vale

1.1 MEASURING TIME

Thursday before Lent	Giovedì grasso	dʒove'di 'grasso
Shrove Tuesday	Martedì grasso	marte'di 'grasso
Ash Wednesday	Mercoledì delle ceneri	merkole'di delle 'tʃeneri
Palm Sunday	Domenica delle Palme	do'menika delle'palme
Holy Week	Settimana Santa	setti'mana 'santa
Maundy Thursday	Giovedì Santo	dʒove'di 'santo
Good Friday	Venerdì Santo	vener'di 'santo
Holy Saturday	Sabato Santo	'sabato 'santo
Easter	Pasqua	'paskwa
Easter Monday	Lunedì dell'Angelo	lune'di del'landʒelo
Labour Day	Festa del lavoro	'fɛsta della'voro
Corpus Christi	Corpus Domini	korpus'domini
Whit Sunday	Pentecoste	pente'kɔste
Feast of the Assumption	Ferragosto	ferra'gosto
All Saints	Ognissanti	oɲɲis'santi
Thanksgiving	Giorno del Ringraziamento	'dʒorno del ringrattsja'mento
Christmas	Natale	na'tale
Boxing Day	Santo Stefano	'santo 'stefano
New Year's Eve	San Silvestro	san sil'vɛstro
holiday	festivo	fes'tivo
weekday	feriale	fe'rjale

■ TEMPORAL ADVERBS AND EXPRESSIONS

always/never	sempre/mai	'sɛmpre/'mai
before/after	prima/dopo	'prima/'dopo
early/late	in anticipo/ in ritardo	inan'titʃipo/ inri'tardo
early/late	presto/tardi	'prɛsto/'tardi
for a short time	per poco tempo	per'pɔko 'tɛmpo

immediately	subito	*'subito*
long ago	tempo fa	*tɛmpo'fa*
next	prossimo	*'prɔssimo*
now	adesso/ora	*a'dɛsso/'ora*
often	spesso	*'spesso*

recently/long ago	da poco/
	   da molto
		*dap'pɔko/
		   dam'molto*

sometimes	qualche volta	*'kwalke 'vɔlta*
soon	fra poco	*frap'pɔko*

blizzard	bufera di neve	*bu'fɛra di'neve*
clear	sereno	*se'reno*
climate	clima	*'klima*
cloudy	nuvoloso	*nuvo'loso*
cold	freddo	*'freddo*
dry	secco	*'sekko*
fog	nebbia	*'nebbja*
hail	grandine	*'grandine*
hot/warm	molto caldo/caldo	*'molto 'kaldo/ 'kaldo*
humid	umido	*'umido*
ice	ghiaccio	*'gjattʃo*
muggy	afoso	*'afoso*
rain	pioggia	*'pjɔddʒa*
snow	neve	*'neve*
storm	temporale	*tempo'rale*
sun	sole	*'sole*
temperature	temperatura	*tempera'tura*
wind	vento	*'vɛnto*

1.2 THE WEATHER

What's the weather like?
Che tempo fa?
It's fine/bad.
Fa bello/brutto.
It's hot/cold.
Fa caldo/freddo.
It's windy.
Tira vento.
It's raining.
Piove.
It's snowing.
Nevica.
There's a mist/fog.
C'è nebbia.
It's clear.
È sereno.
What will the weather be like tomorrow?
Che tempo farà domani?
What's the temperature?
Quanti gradi ci sono?
It's thirty degrees Celsius in the shade.
Ci sono trenta gradi all'ombra.

EXPRESSIONS OF COURTESY

These expressions, among which are listed the usual phrases of courtesy, can be used to complete phrases of any situation as well as the simplest conversation. Don't forget that a request has a better chance of being granted if concluded with the classic "per favore".

Yes.	Sì.	si
No.	No.	nɔ
Yes, please.	Sì, per favore.	si perfa'vore
No, thank you.	No, grazie.	nɔ 'grattsje
Please.	Per favore.	perfa'vore
Thank you.	Grazie.	'grattsje
You're welcome.	Prego.	'prego
Not at all.	Di niente.	di'njɛnte
Excuse me.	Mi scusi.	mis'kuzi
I'm sorry.	Mi dispiace.	midis'pjatʃe
Take a seat.	Si accomodi.	siak'kɔmodi
Come in/ Go ahead.	Passi pure.	'passi 'pure
May I come in? (to enter)	Permesso?	per'messo
Excuse me! (to pass)	Permesso!	per'messo
Come in.	Entri.	'entri
Don't worry.	Non si preoccupi.	'non sipre'ɔkkupi
I'm a foreigner.	Sono straniero.	'sono stra'njɛro
May I ... ?	Potrei ... ?	po'trɛi
Could you ... ?	Potrebbe ... ?	po'trɛbbe

INTERROGATIVES

How much/many?	Quanto? Quanti?	'kwanto kwanti
How?	Come?	'kome
What did he/ she say?	Che ha detto?	ke ad'detto

What did you say?	Come?	'kome
What does it/ that mean?	Che cosa significa?	kek'kɔsa siɲ'nifika
What?	Che cosa?	kek'kɔsa
When?	Quando?	'kwando
Where is it?	Dov'è?	do'vɛ
Where?	Dove?	'dove
Which one is it/he/she?	Qual è?	kwa'lɛ
Which?	Quale?	'kwale
Who is it/he/she?	Chi è?	ki'ɛ
Who?	Chi?	ki
Why?	Perché?	per'ke

■ GREETINGS AND SALUTATIONS

Hello.	Buongiorno.	bwon'dʒorno
Good afternoon/ good evening.	Buonasera.	bwona'sera
Goodnight.	Buona notte.	bwona'nɔtte
Goodbye.	Arrivederci.	arrive'dertʃi
Bye.	Ciao.	'tʃao
Bon voyage/Have a nice trip.	Buon viaggio.	bwɔn vi'addʒo
Good luck.	Buona fortuna.	'bwɔna for'tuna
See you soon.	A presto.	ap'prɛsto
See you later.	A più tardi.	appjut'tardi
Until this evening.	A stasera.	asta'sera
Until tomorrow.	A domani.	addo'mani
Best wishes!	Tanti auguri!	'tanti au'guri
Well done!/ congratulations!	Complimenti!	kompli'menti
Happy birthday!	Buon compleanno!	bwɔn komple'anno
Merry Christmas!	Buon Natale!	bwɔn na'tale
Happy New Year!	Felice anno nuovo!	fe'litʃe 'anno 'nwɔvo

24

Happy Easter!	Buona Pasqua!	'bwɔna 'paskwa
How are you?	Come sta?	'kome sta
Well, thank you, and you?	Bene, grazie e Lei?	'bɛne 'grattʃje el'lɛi
Well.	Bene.	'bɛne
Quite well.	Abbastanza bene.	abbas'tantsa 'bɛne
Not bad.	Non c'è male.	non tʃɛm'male

■ EXPRESSIONS OF APPROVAL AND COMPLIMENTS

Certainly.	Certamente.	tʃerta'mente
Happily.	Volentieri.	volen'tjɛri
Good.	Bene.	'bɛne
Very good.	Benissimo.	be'nissimo
Excellent.	Ottimo.	'ɔttimo
With great pleasure.	Con molto piacere.	kon 'molto pja'tʃere
How nice!	Che bello!	keb'bɛllo
Well done!	Bravo!	'bravo
Indeed.	Vero.	'vero
Right.	Giusto.	'dʒusto
I'm pleased.	Sono contento.	'sɔno kon'tɛnto
That was nice.	Sono stato bene.	sonos'tato 'bɛne
You're right.	Lei ha ragione.	'lɛi arra'dʒone
I like/ liked it.	Mi piace/ mi è piaciuto.	mi'pjatʃe/ mjɛppja'tʃuto

■ EXPRESSIONS OF DISAPPROVAL

Never.	Mai.	'mai
Nothing.	Niente.	'njɛnte
Bad.	Male.	'male
Terrible.	Orribile.	or'ribile
How awful!	Che brutto!	keb'brutto
Unfortunately.	Purtroppo.	pur'trɔppo
I don't agree.	Non sono d'accordo.	non'sɔno dak'kɔrdo

25

1.3 DAILY VOCABULARY

It's wrong.	È sbagliato.	ɛzbaʎˈʎato
Not at all.	Per niente.	perˈnjɛnte
What a pity!	Che peccato!	keppekˈkato
What bad luck!	Che sfortuna!	kesforˈtuna
You're quite wrong.	Lei ha torto.	ˈlɛi atˈtɔrto
I don't like/	Non mi piace/	non miˈpjatʃe/
didn't like it.	non mi è piaciuto.	non mjɛppjaˈtʃuto
I'm dissatisfied.	Sono	ˈsono
	insoddisfatto	insoddisˈfatto
I'm cross/angry.	Sono arrabbiato.	ˈsono arrabˈbjato

■ PERSONAL PRONOUNS (SUBJECT AND OBJECT)

I, me	io, me	ˈio me
you	tu, te	tu te
he, him	egli, lui	ˈeʎʎi, ˈlui
she, her	ella, lei	ˈella, ˈlɛi
it	esso, lui	ˈesso, ˈlui
we, us	noi	ˈnoi
you	voi	ˈvoi
they, them	loro	ˈloro

■ POSSESSIVE ADJECTIVES AND PRONOUNS

my, mine	il mio	ilˈmio
your, yours	il tuo	ilˈtuo
his	il suo	ilˈsuo
her, hers	il suo	ilˈsuo
its	il suo	ilˈsuo
our, ours	il nostro	ilˈnɔstro
your, yours	il vostro	ilˈvɔstro
their, theirs	il loro	ilˈloro
own	il proprio	ilˈprɔprjo

■ ONE HUNDRED IMPORTANT NOUNS

abroad	estero	ˈɛstero
account	conto	ˈkonto
address	indirizzo	indiˈrittso
application	domanda	doˈmanda
appointment	appuntamento	appuntaˈmento
arrival	arrivo	arˈrivo
avenue	viale	viˈale
baggage check	deposito bagagli	deˈpɔzito baˈgaʎʎi
boarding card	carta d'imbarco	ˈkarta dimˈbarko
booking	prenotazione	prenotatˈtsjone
boy/girl	ragazzo/a	raˈgattso/raˈgattsa
brother	fratello	fraˈtɛllo
bus terminal	stazione degli autobus/ dei pullman	statˈtsjone deˈʎʎautobus/ deiˈpulman
business	affari	afˈfari
cancellation	annullamento	annullaˈmento
child	bambino/a	bamˈbino/bamˈbina
city	città	tʃitˈta
confirmation	conferma	konˈferma
connection	coincidenza	kointʃiˈdɛntsa
country	paese	paˈeze
credit card	carta di credito	ˈkarta diˈkredito
currency	valuta	vaˈluta
customs	dogana	doˈgana
delay	ritardo	riˈtardo
departure	partenza	parˈtɛntsa
deposit	deposito	deˈpɔzito
dialling code	prefisso	preˈfisso
embarkation	imbarco	imˈbarko
exchange	cambio	ˈkambjo
exit	uscita	uʃˈʃita
fare	tariffa	taˈriffa
foreigner	straniero	straˈnjɛro

friend	amico/a	a'miko a'mika
holiday	ferie/	'fɛrje/
	vacanza	va'kantsa
house/home	casa	'kasa
husband	marito	ma'rito
identity card	carta d'identità	'karta didenti'ta
information	ufficio	uf'fitʃo
office	informazioni	informat'tsjoni
insurance	assicurazione	assikurat'tsjone
Italian	italiano	ita'ljano
journey	viaggio	vi'addʒo
key	chiave	'kjave
licence	patente	pa'tɛnte
luggage	bagaglio	ba'gaʎʎo
man	uomo	'wɔmo
money	denaro/soldi	de'naro/'sɔldi
name	nome	'nome
nationality	nazionalità	nattsjonali'ta
passport	passaporto	passa'pɔrto
piazza/square	piazza	'pjattsa
piece of	documento	doku'mento
identification		
police	polizia	polit'tsia
porter	facchino	fak'kino
price	prezzo	'prɛttso
receipt	scontrino	skon'trino
reimbursement	rimborso	rim'borso
reply	risposta	ris'posta
return trip	andata e ritorno	an'data erri'torno
seat	sedile	se'dile
seat/place	posto	'posto
service	servizio	ser'vittsjo
sister	sorella	so'rɛlla
smoking/	fumatori/	fuma'tori/
non smoking	non fumatori	nonfuma'tori

son/daughter	figlio/a	'fiʎʎo/'fiʎʎa
state	stato	'stato
station	stazione	stat'tsjone
stay	permanenza	perma'nɛntsa
stopover	scalo	'skalo
street	via	'via
strike	sciopero	'ʃɔpero
student	studente	stu'dɛnte
suitcase	valigia	va'lidʒa
supplement	supplemento	supple'mento
surname	cognome	koɲ'ɲome
taxi rank	stazione dei taxi	stat'tsjone dei'taksi
ticket	biglietto	biʎ'ʎetto
ticket office/ box office	biglietteria	biʎʎette'ria
timetable	orario	o'rarjo
tip	mancia	'mantʃa
toilet	toilette	twa'lɛt
tourist	turista	tu'rista
underground station	stazione della metropolitana	stat'tsjone della metropoli'tana
view	vista	'vista
visa	visto	'visto
waiter/waitress	cameriere/a	kame'rjɛre/a
waiting room	sala d'attesa	'sala dat'tesa
water	acqua	'akkwa
wife	moglie	'moʎʎe
woman	donna	'dɔnna
work/job	lavoro	la'voro

■ USEFUL ADJECTIVES AND ADVERBS AND THEIR OPPOSITES

amusing/boring	divertente/noioso	diver'tɛnte/no'joso
beautiful/ugly	bello/brutto	'bɛllo/'brutto
better/worse	migliore/peggiore	miʎ'ʎore/ped'dʒore

broken/whole	rotto/intero	'rotto/in'tero
certainly/perhaps	certamente/forse	tʃerta'mente/'forse
clean/dirty	pulito/sporco	pu'lito/'spɔrko
dry/wet	asciutto/bagnato	aʃ'ʃutto/baɲ'ɲato
early/late	presto/tardi	'prɛsto/'tardi
easy/difficult	facile/difficile	'fatʃile/dif'fitʃile

enough/
  too much
	abbastanza/
	  troppo
		abbas'tantsa/
		  'trɔppo

enough/more	basta/ancora	'basta/an'kora
everyone/no one	tutti/nessuno	'tutti/nes'suno

everything/
  nothing
	tutto/
	  niente
		'tutto/
		  'njɛnte

expensive/cheap	caro/economico	'karo/eko'nɔmiko

famous/
  unknown
	famoso/
	  sconosciuto
		fa'moso/
		  skonoʃ'ʃuto

far away/near	lontano/vicino	lon'tano/vi'tʃino
fast/slow	veloce/lento	ve'lotʃe/'lɛnto
fat/thin	grasso/magro	'grasso/'magro

feminine/
  masculine
	femminile/
	  maschile
		femmi'nile/
		  mas'kile

for/against	pro/contro	'prɔ/'kontro
free/engaged	libero/occupato	'libero/okku'pato
full/empty	pieno/vuoto	'pjɛno/'vwɔto
good/bad	buono/cattivo	'bwɔno/kat'tivo
happy/sad	allegro/triste	al'legro/'triste
hard/soft	duro/morbido	'duro/'mɔrbido
high/low	alto/basso	'alto/'basso
hot/cold	caldo/freddo	'kaldo/'freddo

intelligent/
  stupid
	intelligente/
	  stupido
		intelli'dʒɛnte/
		  'stupido

kind/unkind	gentile/scortese	dʒen'tile/skor'teze
large/small	grande/piccolo	'grande/'pikkolo
light/dark	chiaro/scuro	'kjaro/'skuro
light/heavy	leggero/pesante	led'dʒɛro/pe'sante
little/much	poco/molto	'pɔko/'molto

USEFUL WORDS FOR TRAVELLING 1.4

many/few	molti/pochi	'molti/'pɔki
new/old	nuovo/vecchio	'nwɔvo/'vɛkkjo
nice/ unpleasant	simpatico/ antipatico	sim'patiko/ anti'patiko
open/closed	aperto/chiuso	a'pɛrto/'kjuso
pleasant/ unpleasant	piacevole/ spiacevole	pja'tʃevole/ spja'tʃevole
public/private	pubblico/privato	'pubbliko/pri'vato
rich/poor	ricco/povero	'rikko/'pɔvero
right/wrong	giusto/sbagliato	'dʒusto/zbaʎʎato
short/long	corto/lungo	'korto/'lungo
simple/ complicated	semplice/ complicato	'semplitʃe/ kompli'kato
strong/weak	forte/debole	'fɔrte/'debole
sufficient/ insufficient	sufficiente/ insufficente	suffi'tʃɛnte/ insuffi'tʃɛnte
sweet/bitter	dolce/amaro	'doltʃe/a'maro
the same/different	uguale/diverso	u'gwale/di'vɛrso
tired/rested	stanco/riposato	'stanko/ripo'sato
true/false	vero/falso	'vero/'falso
useful/useless	utile/inutile	'utile/i'nutile
very good/ very bad	ottimo/ pessimo	'ɔttimo/ 'pɛssimo
wide/narrow	largo/stretto	'largo/'stretto
young/old	giovane/vecchio	'dʒovane/'vɛkkjo

■ THE MOST COMMON VERBS

to arrive	arrivare	arri'vare
to ask	domandare	doman'dare
to be	essere	'ɛssere
to be able	potere	po'tere
to believe	credere	'kredere
to book	prenotare	preno'tare
to buy	comprare	kom'prare
to call/be called	chiamare/chiamarsi	kja'mare/kja'marsi

31

to change	cambiare	*kam'bjare*
to climb (stairs)	salire	*sa'lire*
to come	venire	*ve'nire*
to cross	attraversare	*attraver'sare*
to cut	tagliare	*taʎ'ʎare*
to descend	scendere	*'ʃendere*
to drink	bere	*'bere*
to drive/guide	guidare	*gwi'dare*
to eat	mangiare	*man'dʒare*
to enter	entrare	*en'trare*
to fill	riempire	*riem'pire*
to finish	finire	*fi'nire*
to fix	riparare	*ripa'rare*
to get into (car, bus)	salire	*sa'lire*
to get off/ to get out of	scendere	*'ʃendere*
to get up	alzare/alzarsi	*al'tsare/al'tsarsi*
to go	andare	*an'dare*
to go out	uscire	*uʃ'ʃire*
to have	avere	*a'vere*
to have to	dovere	*do'vere*
to hire	noleggiare	*noled'dʒare*
to know	conoscere/ sapere	*ko'noʃʃere/ sa'pere*
to leave	lasciare/ partire	*laʃ'ʃare/ par'tire*
to lend	prestare	*pres'tare*
to live	abitare/ vivere	*abi'tare/ 'vivere*
to make/to do	fare	*'fare*
to make an appointment	fissare	*fis'sare*
to move	spostarsi	*spos'tarsi*
to order	ordinare	*ordi'nare*

to park	parcheggiare	parked'dʒare
to pass	passare	pas'sare
to pay	pagare	pa'gare
to play (a game)	giocare	dʒo'kare
to play (a musical instrument)	suonare	swo'nare
to please	piacere	pja'tʃere
to put	mettere	'mettere
to read	leggere	'lɛddʒere
to rent/to let	affittare	affit'tare
to reply	rispondere	ris'pondere
to return (give back)	rendere	'rɛndere
to return (to a place)	tornare	tor'nare
to run	correre	'korrere
to say	dire	'dire
to see	vedere	ve'dere
to sit	sedersi	se'dersi
to sleep	dormire	dor'mire
to speak	parlare	par'lare
to spend	spendere	'spɛndere
to stop	sostare/fermare/ fermarsi	sos'tare/fer'mare/ fer'marsi
to take/get/fetch	prendere	'prɛndere
to telephone	telefonare	telefo'nare
to think	pensare	pen'sare
to travel	viaggiare	viad'dʒare
to understand	capire	ka'pire
to visit	visitare	vizi'tare
to wait	aspettare	aspet'tare
to wake up	svegliare/ svegliarsi	zveʎ'ʎare/ zveʎ'ʎarsi
to walk	camminare	kammi'nare
to want	volere	vo'lere

| to wash | lavare | la'vare |
| to write | scrivere | 'skrivere |

VERB EXPRESSIONS

to need	avere bisogno di	a'vere bi'zoɲɲo di
to be hot	avere caldo	a'vere 'kaldo
to be hungry	avere fame	a'vere 'fame
to be cold	avere freddo	a'vere 'freddo
to be in a hurry	avere fretta	a'vere 'fretta
to be afraid of …	avere paura di …	a'vere pa'ura di
to be thirsty	avere sete	a'vere 'sete
to be sleepy	avere sonno	a'vere 'sonno
to feel like	avere voglia di …	a'vere 'vɔʎʎa di
to be late	essere in ritardo	'ɛssere inri'tardo
I am … years old.	Ho … anni.	ɔ … 'anni
to take a walk	fare una passeggiata	'fare unapassed'dʒata
to go	andare	an'dare
to fetch	andare a prendere	an'dare ap'prɛndere
to visit	andare a trovare	an'dare attro'vare
to go to …	andare a …	an'dare a
I like/ don't like	mi piace/ non mi piace	mi'pjatʃe/ nonmi'pjatʃe

DIRECTIONS AND LOCATIONS

across	attraverso	attra'vɛrso
at the beginning/ at the end	all'inizio/ alla fine	alli'nittsjo/ alla'fine
at the top/ at the bottom	in alto/ in basso	i'nalto/ im'basso
at the top/ at the end of	in cima/ in fondo a	in'tʃima/ in'fondo a
central	centrale	tʃen'trale

centre/ surroundings	centro/ periferia	'tʃɛntro/ perife'ria
down/up	giù/su	dʒu/su
far away/ near	lontano/ vicino	lon'tano/ vi'tʃino
here	qui/qua	kwi/kwa
in front of/behind	davanti/dietro	da'vanti/'djɛtro
in the neigh- bourhood of	nelle vicinanze di	nellevitʃi'nan- tse di
into the centre	al centro	al'tʃentro
next to	accanto	ak'kanto
north/south	nord/sud	nɔrd/sud
northern/ southern	settentrionale/ meridionale	settentrjo'nale/ meridjo'nale
on the other side	dall'altra parte	dal'laltra 'parte
on top of/under	sopra/sotto	'sopra/'sotto
opposite of	di fronte a	di'fronte a
straight on	a diritto	addi'ritto
there	lì/là	li/la
to the right/ to the left	a destra/ a sinistra	ad'dɛstra/ assi'nistra
west/east	ovest/est	'ɔvest/ɛst

high tension	alta tensione	'alta ten'sjone
open	aperto	a'pɛrto
lift	ascensore	aʃʃen'sore
beware of the dog	attenti al cane	at'tɛnti al'kane
mind the step	attenti allo scalino	at'tɛnti alloska'lino
ticket office/ box office	biglietteria	biʎʎette'ria
cash desk	cassa	'kassa
closed	chiuso	'kjuso
full	completo	kom'plɛto
entrance	entrata	en'trata
Please come in	entrata libera	en'trata 'libera
out of stock	esaurito	ezau'rito
fire extinguisher	estintore	estin'tore
free (no charge)	gratis	'gratis
out of order	guasto	'gwasto
on sale	in vendita	in'vendita
information	informazioni	informat'tsjoni
work in progress	lavori in corso	la'vori in'korso
vacancy	libero	'libero
do not cross	non attraversare	nonattraver'sare
don't walk on the flower beds	non calpestare le aiuole	nonkalpes'tare lea'jɔle
do not disturb	non disturbare	nondistur'bare
do not touch	non toccare	nontok'kare
occupied/engaged	occupato	okku'pato
hospital	ospedale	ospe'dale
danger	pericolo	pe'rikolo
wet paint	pittura fresca	pit'tura 'freska
reserved	prenotato	preno'tato
private property	proprietà privata	proprje'ta pri'vata
stairs	scale	'skale
escalator	scala mobile	'skala 'mɔbile
ladies	signore	siɲ'ɲore
gentlemen	signori	siɲ'ɲori

silence	silenzio	*si'lɛntsjo*
push	spingere	*'spindʒere*
ring	suonare	*swo'nare*
telephone	telefono	*te'lɛfono*
pull	tirare	*ti'rare*
toilets	toilette	*twa'lɛt*
exit	uscita	*uʃ'ʃita*
emergency exit	uscita	*uʃ'ʃita*
	di emergenza	*diemer'dʒɛntsa*
no smoking	vietato fumare	*vje'tato fu'mare*
no entry	vietato l'ingresso	*vje'tato lin'grɛsso*
do not	vietato lasciare	*vje'tato laʃ'ʃare*
litter	rifiuti	*ri'fjuti*

■ CARDINAL NUMBERS

0	zero	'dzɛro
1	uno	'uno
2	due	'due
3	tre	tre
4	quattro	'kwattro
5	cinque	'tʃinkwe
6	sei	'sɛi
7	sette	'sette
8	otto	'ɔtto
9	nove	'nɔve
10	dieci	'djɛtʃi
11	undici	'unditʃi
12	dodici	'doditʃi
13	tredici	'treditʃi
14	quattordici	kwat'torditʃi
15	quindici	'kwinditʃi
16	sedici	'seditʃi
17	diciassette	ditʃas'sette
18	diciotto	di'tʃɔtto
19	diciannove	ditʃan'nɔve
20	venti	'venti
21	ventuno	ven'tuno
22	ventidue	venti'due
23	ventitré	venti'tre
24	ventiquattro	venti'kwattro
25	venticinque	venti'tʃinkwe
30	trenta	'trenta
35	trentacinque	trenta'tʃinkwe
40	quaranta	kwa'ranta
50	cinquanta	tʃin'kwanta
60	sessanta	ses'santa
70	settanta	set'tanta
80	ottanta	ot'tanta
90	novanta	no'vanta

100	cento	'tʃɛnto
101	centouno	tʃɛnto'uno
102	centodue	tʃɛnto'due
105	centocinque	tʃɛnto'tʃinkwe
110	centodieci	tʃɛnto'djɛtʃi
120	centoventi	tʃɛnto'venti
125	centoventicinque	tʃɛntoventi'tʃinkwe
130	centotrenta	tʃɛnto'trenta
150	centocinquanta	tʃɛntotʃin'kwanta
156	centocinquantasei	tʃɛntotʃinkwanta'sɛi
200	duecento	due'tʃɛnto
400	quattrocento	kwattro'tʃɛnto
500	cinquecento	tʃinkwe'tʃɛnto
600	seicento	sɛi'tʃɛnto
700	settecento	sɛtte'tʃɛnto
900	novecento	nɔve'tʃɛnto
1000	mille	'mille
1208	milleduecentootto	milleduetʃɛnto'ɔtto
2000	duemila	due'mila
5563	cinquemilacinque-centosessantatré	tʃinkwemilatʃinkwet-ʃɛntosessanta'tre
10,000	diecimila	djɛtʃi'mila
20,000	ventimila	venti'mila
35,648	trentacinquemila-seicento-quarantotto	trentatʃinkwemila-sɛitʃɛnto kwaran'tɔtto
100,000	centomila	tʃɛnto'mila
200,000	duecentomila	duetʃɛnto'mila
1,000,000	un milione	unmi'ljone
1,000,000,000	un miliardo	unmi'ljardo
3.14	tre e quattordici	tre ekkwat'torditʃi
5.6	cinque virgola sei	'tʃinkwe 'virgolas'sɛi
7/12	sette dodicesimi	'sɛtte dodi'tʃɛzimi

39

12%	dodici per cento	'doditʃi per'tʃɛnto
half	metà (di)	me'ta di
a quarter	un quarto	un'kwarto
ten	una diecina	unadje'tʃina
a dozen	una dozzina	unadod'dzina
a hundred	un centinaio	untʃenti'najo
a thousand	un migliaio	unmiʎ'ʎajo
double	doppio	'doppjo
once	una volta	una'vɔlta
twice	due volte	due'vɔlte
a couple of …	un paio di …	um'pajo di
3 plus 2	tre più due	tre pjud'due
8 minus 5	otto meno cinque	'ɔtto meno'tʃinkwe
3 times 4	tre moltiplicato quattro	tre moltipli'kato 'kwattro
6 divided by 2	sei diviso due	'sɛi di'vizo 'due

■ ORDINAL NUMBERS

1st	primo	'primo
2nd	secondo	se'kondo
3rd	terzo	'tɛrtso
4th	quarto	'kwarto
5th	quinto	'kwinto
6th	sesto	'sɛsto
7th	settimo	'sɛttimo
8th	ottavo	ot'tavo
9th	nono	'nɔno
10th	decimo	'dɛtʃimo
11th	undicesimo	undi'tʃɛzimo
12th	dodicesimo	dodi'tʃɛzimo
13th	tredicesimo	tredi'tʃɛzimo
14th	quattordicesimo	kwattordi'tʃɛzimo
15th	quindicesimo	kwindi'tʃɛzimo
16th	sedicesimo	sedi'tʃɛzimo
17th	diciassettesimo	ditʃasset'tɛzimo

18th	diciottesimo	ditʃot'tɛzimo
19th	diciannovesimo	ditʃanno'vezimo
20th	ventesimo	ven'tɛzimo
21st	ventunesimo	ventu'nɛzimo
22nd	ventiduesimo	ventidu'ɛzimo
23rd	ventitreesimo	ventitre'ɛzimo
24th	ventiquattresimo	ventikwat'trɛzimo
25th	venticinquesimo	ventitʃin'kwɛzimo
30th	trentesimo	tren'tɛzimo
70th	settantesimo	settan'tɛzimo
80th	ottantesimo	ottan'tɛzimo
90th	novantesimo	novan'tɛzimo
100th	centesimo	tʃen'tɛzimo
500th	cinquecentesimo	tʃinkwetʃen'tɛzimo
1,000th	millesimo	mil'lɛzimo
10,000th	diecimillesimo	djɛtʃimil'lɛzimo
one millionth	milionesimo	miljo'nɛzimo

Here are a few examples of how to formulate a price:

It costs 10 euro.
Costa dieci euro.
It costs 22 euro.
Costa ventidue euro.

■ WEIGHTS AND MEASURES

gross weight	peso lordo	'peso 'lordo
net weight	peso netto	'peso 'netto
tare	tara	'tara
ton	tonnellata	tonnel'lata
a hundred kilos	quintale	kwin'tale
kilogramme	chilogrammo	kilo'grammo
a hundred grammes	ettogrammo	ɛtto'grammo
gramme	grammo	'grammo
milligramme	milligrammo	milli'grammo

pound (lb)	libbra	'libbra
ounce (oz)	oncia	'ontʃa
How much does it weigh?		
Quanto pesa?		'kwanto 'pesa
litre	litro	'litro
half a litre	mezzo litro	'mɛddzo 'litro
one-tenth of a litre	decilitro	de'tʃilitro
gallon	gallone	gal'lone
pint	pinta	'pinta
How much does it contain?		
Quanto contiene?		'kwanto kon'tjɛne
kilometre	chilometro	ki'lɔmetro
metre	metro	'mɛtro
centimetre	centimetro	tʃen'timetro
millimetre	millimetro	mil'limetro
mile	miglio terrestre	'miʎʎo ter'rɛstre
nautical mile	miglio marino	'miʎʎo ma'rino
foot	piede	'pjɛde
inch	pollice	'pɔllitʃe
knot	nodo	'nɔdo
How long is it?	Quanto è lungo?	'kwanto ɛ'lungo
How far is it?	Quanto dista?	'kwanto 'dista
acre	acro	'akro
square metre	metro quadrato	'mɛtro kwa'drato
cubic metre	metro cubo	'mɛtro 'kubo
hectare	ettaro	'ɛttaro

■ TEMPERATURE

degrees centigrade	gradi centigradi	'gradi tʃen'tigradi
degrees Fahrenheit	gradi Fahrenheit	'gradi 'farenait
What is the temperature?		'kwanti 'gradi
Quanti gradi sono?		'sono

beige	beige	*bɛʒ*
black	nero	*'nero*
blue	azzurro/	*ad'dzurro/*
	blu	*blu*
brown	marrone	*mar'rone*
gold	oro	*'ɔro*
green	verde	*'verde*
grey	grigio	*'gridʒo*
lilac	lilla	*'lilla*
metallic	metallizzato	*metallid'dzato*
ochre	ocra	*'ɔkra*
orange	arancio	*a'rantʃo*
phosphorescent	fosforescente	*fosforeʃ'ʃɛnte*
pink	rosa	*'rɔza*
purple	porpora	*'porpora*
red	rosso	*'rosso*
silver	argento	*ar'dʒɛnto*
violet	viola	*vi'ɔla*
white	bianco	*'bjanko*
yellow	giallo	*'dʒallo*
brilliant	brillante	*bril'lante*
dark	scuro	*'skuro*
light	chiaro	*'kjaro*
opaque/dull	opaco	*o'pako*

1.8 SPECIAL NEEDS

■ SMOKING (AND NON-SMOKING)

May I smoke?
Posso fumare?
Where is the smoking/non-smoking area?
Dov'è la zona fumatori/non fumatori?
Would you like a cigarette?
Vuole una sigaretta?
Do you have a cigarette/light?
Ha una sigaretta/da accendere?
The smoke annoys me.
Mi disturba il fumo.
You are not allowed to smoke in this area.
In questa zona è vietato fumare.

■ THE DISABLED

Are there access ramps for the disabled?
Ci sono rampe di accesso per disabili?
Are there toilets for the disabled?
Ci sono bagni per disabili?
Are there lifts in the building?
Ci sono ascensori nell'edificio?
Can a wheelchair be taken into the lift?
È possibile introdurre una sedia a rotelle nell'ascensore?
Can you help me please?
Mi può aiutare?
Are there reductions for the disabled?
Ci sono riduzioni per disabili?

■ CHILDREN

cot	lettino	*let'tino*
crib	culla	*'kulla*
newborn infant	neonato	*neo'nato*
pram	carrozzina	*karrot'tsina*
push-chair	passeggino	*passed'dʒino*

Are there discounts/reductions for children under 4/12?
Ci sono facilitazioni/riduzioni sotto i quattro/dodici anni?
Where can I warm the baby's bottle?
Dove posso riscaldare il biberon?
Where can I change the baby?
Dove posso cambiare il bambino?
Where can I sterilize … ?
Dove posso sterilizzare … ?
I am travelling with a child of three.
Viaggio con un bambino di tre anni.
Does one pay the full price for the baby?
Il bambino paga per intero?
The baby sits on my lap.
Il bambino si siede sulle mie ginocchia.
Can you please bring me a highchair?
Mi può portare un seggiolone?
I would like a babysitter for today/this evening.
Vorrei una babysitter per oggi/stasera.
Are there play areas for children?
Ci sono aree per l'intrattenimento dei bambini?
Is there a playground?
C'è un parco-giochi?

■ TRAVELLING WITH PETS
Are dogs allowed in?
È permesso l'ingresso ai cani?
Can I keep a dog in the flat/suite/room?
Posso tenere un cane nell'appartamento/in camera?

È vietato l'ingresso agli animali.
No animals allowed.

Does one pay for a ticket for pets too?
Pagano il biglietto anche gli animali?

1.8 SPECIAL NEEDS

Where are the kennels?
Dov'è il canile?
The cat travels in its cage.
Il gatto viaggia nella sua gabbia.
May I let the dog free in the park?
Posso lasciare il cane libero nel parco?

Il cane va tenuto al guinzaglio.
Dogs must be on a lead.

Il cane deve avere la museruola.
Dogs must wear muzzles.

May I take the dog on the beach?
Posso portare il cane sulla spiaggia?
He/she is friendly: he/she won't bite!
È buono, non morde!
I have the vaccination certificate.
Ho il certificato delle vaccinazioni.
May I leave the dog here for a moment?
I'll be back immediately.
Posso lasciare il cane qui per un momento?
Torno subito.

AREA 2. TRAVELLING

In this Area we have gathered the words and phrases relative to your journey or getting from one place to another. Naturally, we have considered not only the trip to Italy, itself, but also the short and long distances that might be covered in excursions or trips throughout the country and using varied means of transport; hence, you will find the phrases necessary for reserving a seat, paying for a ticket, renting a vehicle, asking for information in airports and stations regarding timetables and services on board, or for registering complaints in the case of poor service. This Area also presents the frequently used words and expressions that arise in crucial moments such as passing through customs and passport control, being pulled over for a traffic violation, ordering small repairs or checks on hired vehicles, and requesting documents, visas and permits in Italian public offices.

2.1
ON THE PLANE AND IN THE AIRPORT

2.2
IN THE CAR OR ON A MOTORCYCLE

2.3
ON THE FERRY BOAT, SHIP, HYDROPLANE

2.4
ON THE TRAIN

2.5
USING PUBLIC TRANSPORT

2.6
DOCUMENTS AND PUBLIC OFFICES

2.7
HIRING A CAR AND OTHER VEHICLES

2.1 ON THE PLANE AND IN THE AIRPORT

IN THE AIRPORT: CHECK-IN AND BOARDING

| **aeroplane** | aeroplano | *aero'plano* |
| **airport** | aeroporto | *aero'pɔrto* |

■ COMMON SIGNS IN AIRPORTS

baggage claim	ritiro bagagli	*ri'tiro ba'gaʎʎi*
boarding gate	porta d'imbarco	*'pɔrta dim'barko*
check-in counter	check-in	*tʃe'kin*
customs	dogana	*do'gana*
gate	cancello	*kan'tʃello*
international/ domestic flights	voli internazionali/ nazionali	*'voli internattsjo'nali/ nattsjo'nali*
passport check point	controllo passaporti	*kon'trollo passa'pɔrti*
waiting room/lounge	sala d'attesa	*'sala dat'tesa*

The following phrases may be useful for both domestic and international flights, whether you have yet to acquire your ticket or not.

Can you tell me where the international/domestic flights are?
Dove sono i voli internazionali/nazionali?

Can you tell me where the [airline] check-in desk is for flight number … ?
Dov'è il check-in del volo [compagnia] per … ?

What time is the next flight for … due to leave?
A che ora parte il prossimo volo per … ?

I'd like to book/confirm a/two seat/s in the name of … on flight … for … .
Vorrei prenotare/confermare un/due … posto/i a nome … sul volo … per … .

A return/An open return/A one-way single ticket for … .
Un biglietto di andata e ritorno/con ritorno aperto/di sola andata per … .

I'd like a smoker's/non-smoker's/central/window/aisle seat, please.
Vorrei un posto fumatori/non fumatori/centrale/vicino al finestrino/al corridoio.

Are there any special/weekend rates?
Ci sono tariffe speciali/weekend?

I'd like to bring forward/delay my departure.
Vorrei anticipare/posticipare la partenza.

> **Il suo biglietto, prego.**
> Your ticket, please.

Is there a connecting flight for … ?
C'è un volo in coincidenza per … ?

How long does the flight take?
Quanto dura il volo?

I'm travelling with a … -year-old child.
Viaggio con un bambino di … anni.

I require the diabetic/vegetarian menu.
Ho bisogno di un menu per diabetici/vegetariani.

I'd like to forward my luggage as far as … .
Vorrei instradare il bagaglio fino a … .

May I take this bag/box into the cabin as hand luggage?
Posso imbarcare questa borsa/scatola come bagaglio a mano?

> **Ha altro bagaglio?**
> Have you got any more luggage?
> **Deve pagare … di sovrappeso.**
> You will have to pay … for the excess weight.
> **Questa è la sua carta d'imbarco, cancello … .**
> Here is your boarding card, Gate … .

■ ANNOUNCEMENTS YOU MAY HEAR ON THE LOUDSPEAKER

> **Il volo … subirà un ritardo di … minuti/ore causa nebbia/maltempo/sciopero.**
> Owing to fog/bad weather/strike action, flight number … will be delayed … minutes/hours.

2.1 ON THE PLANE AND IN THE AIRPORT

Il volo … per … è stato cancellato.
Flight number … for … has been cancelled.
Passeggeri del volo … per … , portarsi al cancello … .
Will passengers holding boarding cards for flight …
please proceed to Gate … .

ON THE PLANE

Some phrases for your needs or curiosity during the flight.

I can't manage to fasten my safety belt.
Non riesco ad allacciarmi la cintura di sicurezza.
When are we due to land?
A che ora è previsto l'atterraggio?
What altitude are we flying at?
A quale altitudine stiamo volando?
I have not received my lunch tray.
Non ho avuto il vassoio del pranzo.
Do you stock duty-free goods on board?
Avete generi duty-free a bordo?
I'd like something for air sickness/nausea, please.
Vorrei qualcosa contro il mal d'aria/la nausea.

■ SIGNS YOU MAY SEE AND ANNOUNCEMENTS YOU MAY HEAR
ON THE PLANE

Il decollo/l'atterraggio è previsto fra … minuti.
We'll be taking off/landing in … minutes.
Allacciare le cinture di sicurezza.
Please fasten your seat belts.
**Stiamo attraversando un'area di turbolenze. È possibile
incontrare vuoti d'aria.**
I'm afraid we have hit some turbulence. We may run into a
few air pockets.
**Si prega di rimanere seduti ai propri posti con le cinture
di sicurezza allacciate e di non fumare.**
Please remain seated with your seat belts fastened and
refrain from smoking.

ARRIVING AT DESTINATION

Where does the luggage of flight ... from ... come through?
Dove arrivano i bagagli del volo ... proveniente da ... ?
Where are the luggage trolleys, please?
Dove sono i carrelli per i bagagli?
Where is the left-luggage office, please?
Dov'è il deposito bagagli?
My luggage has not arrived. Who can I speak to about it? I was on flight ... from ... .
Il mio bagaglio non è arrivato: a chi mi debbo rivolgere? Ero sul volo ... da ... .
My suitcase has been opened/damaged.
La mia valigia è stata aperta/danneggiata.

> **Deve riempire questo modulo.**
> Please fill in this form.

■ CUSTOMS

Here we present the phrases relative to the control of both passports and baggage. European Union norms have abolished customs checks for citizens of EU countries, but it is still necessary to show a valid Personal Identification document at borders. If you are travelling from a non-EU country to Italy, it is obligatory to declare only those articles acquired in the country of origin at customs. If you are travelling with only personal effects or gifts that respect the Italian customs laws, then you have "Niente da dichiarare" (nothing to declare).

> **I suoi documenti, prego.**
> Your papers, please.
> **Qual è il motivo del suo viaggio?**
> What is the reason for your journey?

It is a business/pleasure/study trip.
È un viaggio di lavoro/turismo/studio.

> **Quanto tempo si trattiene nel paese?**
> How long are you intending to stay?

2.1 ON THE PLANE AND IN THE AIRPORT

Ha qualcosa/niente da dichiarare?
Have you anything to declare?

Nothing to declare.
Niente da dichiarare.
I have a ... for my personal use.
Ho un ... per uso personale.

Può aprire questa valigia/borsa/scatola?
Would you open this suitcase/bag/box, please?

LEAVING THE AIRPORT

Can you tell me where the exit is, please?
Dov'è l'uscita?
Where is a foreign exchange counter?
Dov'è l'ufficio cambio?
Where is the tourist information office?
Dov'è l'ufficio informazioni turistiche?
Can you tell me where I can hire a car?
Dov'è l'autonoleggio?
Which is the cheapest way to get into the centre?
Qual è il modo più economico per raggiungere il centro?
Is there a train/bus/underground line for the city?
C'è un treno/un autobus/una linea del metrò per la città?
Which route does the coach take?
Qual è il tragitto del pullman?
Can you tell me where the ticket office is, please?
Dov'è la biglietteria?
Can you tell me where the stop is, please?
Dov'è la fermata?
Can you tell me where the taxi rank is, please?
Dov'è la stazione dei taxi?

IN THE CAR OR ON A MOTORCYCLE 2.2

In this section you will find the words and phrases that are useful for travelling by car, facing the normal situations (including some small emergencies) that arise when moving on 4 (or 2) wheels. Accidents and serious breakdowns are not presented here (see Situation 4.1) nor is theft (4.2). To rent a car or other means of transport, see Situation 2.7.

■ PERSONAL AND CAR DOCUMENTS

car insurance certificate	contrassegno assicurazione	*kontras'seɲɲo assikurat'tsjone*
driving licence	patente	*pa'tɛnte*
green card	carta verde	*'karta 'verde*
registration document	libretto di circolazione	*li'bretto ditʃirkolat'tsjone*
registration plate	targa	*'targa*
road licence	bollo	*'bollo*

■ SIGNS YOU MAY SEE AT COUNTRY BORDERS AND TOLL BOOTHS

Customs	Dogana	*dógana*
Frontier	Confine di Stato	*kon'fine dis'tato*
... km to border	Frontiera a ... km	*fron'tjɛra a ki'lɔmetri*
Take a ticket	Ritirare il biglietto	*riti'rare ilbiʎ'ʎetto*
Toll	Pedaggio	*pe'daddʒo*
Tollgate	Casello	*ka'sɛllo*

■ POSSIBLE REQUESTS AT CUSTOMS

Ha niente da dichiarare?
Have you anything to declare?
Apra il bagagliaio.
Open the boot.
Apra quella borsa/scatola/valigia.
Open that bag/box/suitcase.

53

Mi mostri la patente/il libretto di circolazione.
May I see your driving licence/registration document?

Where may I get a green card?
Dove posso fare la carta verde?

■ VEHICLES

car	automobile	auto'mɔbile
saloon car	berlina	ber'lina
coupé	coupé	ku'pe
estate wagon	familiare	fami'ljare
all terrain vehicle	fuoristrada	fwɔris'trada
roadster	spider	'spaider
bicycle	bicicletta	bitʃi'kletta
moped	ciclomotore	tʃiklomo'tore
motor cycle	motocicletta	mototʃi'kletta
motor scooter	motorino	moto'rino
trailer	rimorchio	ri'mɔrkjo
caravan	caravan	'karavan

■ VARIOUS CATEGORIES OF ROADS AND TRAFFIC

carriageway	carreggiata	karred'dʒata
central reservation/ median	spartitraffico	sparti'traffiko
dual carriage way	superstrada	supers'trada
emergency box	colonnina di soccorso	kolon'nina disok'korso
exit	uscita	uʃ'ʃita
junction/crossing	svincolo	'zvinkolo
lane	corsia	kor'sia
escape lane	di emergenza	diemer'dʒɛntsa
overtaking lane	di sorpasso	disor'passo
link road	raccordo	rak'kɔrdo
motorway	autostrada	autos'trada
road	strada	'strada
trunk road	nazionale	nattsjo'nale

regional road	provinciale	*provin'tʃale*
dirt road	vicinale	*vitʃi'nale*
road assistance	soccorso	*sok'korso*
	stradale	*stra'dale*
stop signal	stop	*stɔp*
traffic lights	semaforo	*se'mafaro*

DIRECTIONS IN CAR TRAVEL

*These phrases are useful to ask for directions while on journey.
Drivers will already be using a road map to get their bearings, hence
the brevity of this section. For bearings and road signs in the city, see
Situation 4.3.*

Excuse me, is the motorway this way?
Vado bene per l'autostrada?
Which is the road for ..., please?
Qual è la strada per … ?
Does it have two/four lanes?
È a due/quattro corsie?
Is the road asphalted?
È una strada asfaltata?

ROAD SIGNS

*Road signs in Italy comply to international standards and norms and
therefore differ little from those of other countries (particularly within
Europe). Having been made to be understood "on sight", it is always
easy to comprehend their meanings. However, should you have difficulty in deciphering a sign, you can always ask someone its meaning.
Road signs are also frequently accompanied by phrases; here are a few
examples:*

access restricted	zona traffico	*'dzɔna 'traffiko*
	limitato	*limi'tato*
avalanche	valanghe	*va'lange*

2.2 IN THE CAR OR ON A MOTORCYCLE

avoid unnecessary noise	zona del silenzio	'dzɔna delsi'lɛntsjo
danger	pericolo	pe'rikolo
detour	deviazione	devjat'tsjone
faulty road surface	strada deformata	'strada defor'mata
fog banks	banchi di nebbia	'banki di'nebbja
heavy plant crossing	uscita autocarri	uʃ'ʃita auto'karri
highway patrol	polizia stradale	polit'tsia stra'dale
ice	ghiaccio	'gjattʃo
keep to the right	serrare a destra	ser'rare ad'dɛstra
landslide	frana	'frana
no	divieto	di'vjɛto
** entry**	di accesso	diat'tʃɛsso
** thoroughfare**	di circolazione	ditʃirkolat'tsjone
** U turns**	d'inversione a U	dinver'sjone a'u
** overtaking**	di sorpasso	disor'passo
park and display	zona disco	'dzɔna 'disko
** time**	orario	o'rarjo
pedestrian precinct	zona pedonale	'dzɔna pedo'nale
possible queue hazard	possibilità di code	possibili'ta di'kode
road closed	strada interrotta	'strada inter'rotta
signs being repainted	segnaletica in rifacimento	seɲɲa'lɛtika inrifatʃi'mento
slippery road	strada sdrucciolevole	'strada zdruttʃo'levole
slow	rallentare	rallen'tare

IN THE CAR OR ON A MOTORCYCLE 2.2

switch off engine when stationary	spegnere il motore in sosta	'speɲɲere ilmo'tore in'sɔsta
switch on head lamps	accendere i fari	at'tʃɛndere i'fari
tunnel	galleria	galle'ria
use of chains compulsory	obbligo di catene	'ɔbbligo dika'tene
works under way	lavori in corso	la'vori in'korso

AT THE SERVICE STATION

■ REFUELLING AND MINOR REPAIRS

battery	batteria	batte'ria
bolt	bullone	bul'lone
car-jack	cric	krik
coupons	coupons	ku'pon
filling up	rifornimento	riforni'mento
inner tube	camera d'aria	'kamera 'darja
mechanic	meccanico	mek'kaniko
nut	dado	'dado
repairs	riparazioni	riparat'tsjoni
screw driver	cacciavite	kattʃa'vite
spanner	chiave inglese	'kjave in'glese
tool kit	cassetta attrezzi	kas'setta at'trettsi
tyre	pneumatico	pneu'matiko

Please put … litres/fill up with …
Metta … litri/il pieno di …
   … leadfree (green) petrol.
   … benzina senza piombo
      (verde).
   … diesel fuel.
   … gasolio.
   … % fuel mixture.
   … miscela al … %.

... super/four-star petrol.
... super.
Please check ...
Mi controlli ...

... the water/cooling liquid.
... l'acqua/il liquido refrigerante.
... the brake fluid.
... l'olio dei freni.
... the engine oil.
... l'olio del motore.
... the battery.
... la batteria.
... the tyre pressure.
... la pressione dei pneumatici.
... the pressure in the spare wheel.
... la pressione della ruota di scorta.
... the brake discs.
... le pasticche dei freni.

■ THE SERVICE STATION ATTENDANT OR MECHANIC MIGHT SAY:

Manca olio. Debbo aggiungerlo?
The oil's rather low. Shall I top it up?
Bisogna cambiare l'olio.
The oil needs changing.
Bisogna sostituire il filtro dell'aria/dell'olio.
The air/oil filter needs replacing.
Aggiungo acqua o liquido?
Shall I add water or liquid?
Bisogna cambiare le candele.
The spark plugs need changing.

Can you tell me if there is a repair garage/car wash/tyre repairer near here?
C'è un'autofficina/un autolavaggio/un gommaio?

IN THE CAR OR ON A MOTORCYCLE 2.2

I have a flat tyre.
Ho una gomma a terra.

> **Bisogna cambiare la camera d'aria.**
> The inner tube will have to be changed.
> **Ci vuole un pneumatico nuovo.**
> A new tyre is needed.

I need to change a fuse/a bulb.
Debbo sostituire un fusibile/una lampadina.

PARKING

break-down lorry	carro-attrezzi	'karro at'trettsi
clamps	ganasce	ga'naʃʃe
fine	multa	'multa
no	divieto	di'vjɛto
stopping	di fermata	difer'mata
waiting	di sosta	di'sɔsta
waiting	di sosta	di'sɔsta
at any time	permanente	perma'nɛnte
parking	parcheggio	par'keddʒo
limited parking	a tempo	at'tɛmpo
pay parking	a pagamento	appaga'mento
parking meter	parchimetro	par'kimetro
pavement	marciapiede	martʃa'pjɛde
tow away zone	rimozione	rimot'tsjone
	forzata	for'tsata
traffic offence	contravvenzione	kontravven'tsjone
vehicle	passo	'passo
passage-way	carrabile	kar'rabile

Is parking allowed here?
Si può parcheggiare qui?
How long can I park here for?
Quanto tempo posso parcheggiare qui?

2.2 IN THE CAR OR ON A MOTORCYCLE

Where is there a tended car park, please?
Dov'è un parcheggio custodito?
What is the hourly/the daily charge?
Quanto costa all'ora/al giorno?
Who is authorized to remove the clamps?
Chi può aprire le ganasce?

> **Deve chiamare un vigile.**
> You will have to call a policeman.

Where can I find a policeman?
Dov'è un vigile?

> **Deve pagare una multa di … . Paga subito?**
> You will have to pay a fine of … . Are you going to pay now?

My car has been towed away. How do I get it back?
La mia auto è stata rimossa. Come posso recuperarla?

> **La sua auto si trova … .**
> Your car is … .

Why have I been fined?
Perché mi avete fatto la multa?

> **La sua macchina è in sosta vietata.**
> Your car is in a no parking area.
> **Questo parcheggio è riservato.**
> This car park is reserved.
> **Il parchimetro è scaduto.**
> The parking meter has expired.
> **Ostruisce il passaggio.**
> It is obstructing the traffic.

■ TRAFFIC VIOLATIONS
We list below, with the hope that they will never be of use, some requests or comments that could be made by traffic police in case you commit a violation or in routine controls.

IN THE CAR OR ON A MOTORCYCLE 2.2

Lei è in contravvenzione.
You are infringing traffic regulations.
Posso vedere ...
May I see ...
... la sua patente/patente internazionale?
... your (international) driving licence?
... il libretto di circolazione?
... your registration book?
... il bollo e l'assicurazione dell'auto?
... your road licence and car insurance?
... la carta verde?
... your green card?
Questa/o patente/documento non è valida/o.
This licence/document is not valid.
Le cinture di sicurezza sono obbligatorie.
Seat belts are compulsory.
Lei è passato con il semaforo rosso.
You crossed on a red light.
Lei ha superato il limite di velocità.
You were exceeding the speed limit.
Lei non ha rispettato lo stop/la precedenza.
You failed to stop at the sign/give way.
Lei ha superato la linea continua.
You went over the continuous line.
Lei viaggiava contromano.
You were travelling on the wrong side of the road.
Questa è una zona pedonale.
This is a pedestrian precinct.
Questa strada è a senso unico.
This is a one-way street.
Questa strada è a traffico limitato.
Traffic is limited in this street.

2.3 ON THE FERRY BOAT, SHIP, HYDROPLANE

AT THE PORT AND ON BOARD

Ferry boat	Traghetto	*tra'getto*
Harbour	Porto	*'pɔrto*
Hydroplane	Aliscafo	*alis'kafo*
Ship	Nave	*'nave*

■ AT THE PORT
Excuse me, where do the ferries/hydroplanes for … leave from?
Da dove partono i traghetti/gli aliscafi per … ?

   Dalla banchina/dal molo ….
   From quay/pier … .

Can you tell me where the ferry/hydroplane from … docks?
Dove attracca il traghetto/aliscafo da … ?
Where is (the company's) information office/ticket office?
Dov'è l'ufficio informazioni/biglietteria della compagnia …?
I'd like the ferry time-table and tariffs for … , please.
Vorrei l'orario e le tariffe dei traghetti per … .
How long does the crossing take?
Quanto dura la traversata?

■ AT THE TICKET OFFICE
How much does the ticket cost …
Quanto costa il biglietto …

   … for an adult/a child?
   … per adulti/bambini?
   … for a single/double/triple cabin?
   … in cabina singola/doppia/tripla?
   … for a seat on deck?
   … in passaggio ponte?
   … for a seat in a reclining armchair?
   … in poltrona reclinabile?
   … for a car?
   … per le auto?

62

... for a bicycle?
... per le biciclette?
... for a motorcycle?
... per le moto?
... for a caravan?
... per le roulotte?
... for a camper?
... per i camper?
... for a trailer?
... per il carrello rimorchio?
How much is a return ticket?
Quanto costa l'andata e ritorno?
May I have the return date left open?
Posso avere il ritorno con data aperta?
I'd like to book ... on the ... (time) ferry for ... (place) ... .
Vorrei prenotare sul traghetto/sull'aliscafo delle ... per ...
    ... deck seats/armchairs/a cabin for ...
    ... il passaggio ponte/la poltrona/la cabina per ...
    ... one/two/three adults plus ...
    ... un/due/tre adulto/i più ...
    ... one child/two/three children plus ...
    ... un/due/tre bambino/i più ...
    ... a car/a motorcycle/a camper ...
    ... un'auto/una moto/un camper.
What time can passengers start boarding?
A che ora inizia l'imbarco?
Is there a bar/restaurant on board?
C'è il bar/ristorante a bordo?

Per la corsa notturna è obbligatorio prenotare la cabina o la poltrona reclinabile.
The reservation of a cabin or reclining armchair is compulsory on the night crossing.
Se viaggia con l'auto deve prenotare anche il ritorno.
When travelling by car, the return journey must be reserved as well.

2.3 ON THE FERRY BOAT, SHIP, HYDROPLANE

■ **ON BOARD**

The following phrases correspond to possible comments on behalf of the personnel or, more likely, to announcements over loudspeakers in the garage of the ferry. As such announcements usually deal with safety regulations, it is wise to pay close attention.

Chiudere le bombole del gas sui camper.
Gas cylinders in campers must be kept closed.
Lasciare la marcia inserita e il freno a mano tirato.
Leave vehicle in gear with the hand brake engaged.
Spengere il motore e togliere le chiavi.
Switch off the engine and remove the keys.
Non chiudere gli sportelli a chiave.
Do not lock your vehicle doors.
Vietato sostare nel garage durante la traversata.
Access to the garage is not permitted during the crossing.

Please can you tell me where ... is/are?
Dov'è/sono ...
>   **... cabin/seat number ...**
>   ... la cabina/poltrona numero ... ?
>   **... the purser's office ...**
>   ... l'ufficio del commissario di bordo?
>   **... the cabin keys ...**
>   ... le chiavi delle cabine?
>   **... the toilets ...**
>   ... la toilette?
>   **... the bar/restaurant/self-service restaurant ...**
>   ... il bar/ristorante/self-service?
>   **... the sick-bay ...**
>   ... l'infermeria?

How do you get to the upper/lower deck?
Come si raggiunge il ponte superiore/inferiore?
I feel sea-sick.
Ho mal di mare.

ON THE FERRY BOAT, SHIP, HYDROPLANE 2.3

My cabin ...
La mia cabina ...

    ... has already been taken.
    ... è già occupata.
    ... is noisy. I'd like to change it.
    ... è rumorosa, vorrei cambiarla.

My cabin door will not open.
La mia cabina non si apre.

The porthole in my cabin will not open.
Nella mia cabina non si apre l'oblò.

On all ferries you will find instruction cards on what to do in case of an emergency posted on board in several languages and with the support of illustrative graphics. In any case, we list below some of the expressions you will find on those signs:

abandon ship	abbandonare la nave	abbando'nare la'nave
fire on board	incendio a bordo	in'tsɛndjo ab'bordo
lifebelt	salvagente	salva'dʒɛnte
lifeboat	scialuppa	ʃa'luppa
man overboard	uomo in mare	'wɔmo in'mare
meeting point	punto di raccolta	'punto dirak'kɔlta
siren/whistle	sirena	si'rɛna

2.4 ON THE TRAIN

AT THE TRAIN STATION

■ INFORMATION, TICKETS AND RESERVATIONS

express train	espresso	*es'presso*
non-stop/ extra fare train	rapido	*'rapido*
regional train	regionale	*redʒo'nale*
stopping train	locale	*lo'kale*
through train	diretto	*di'retto*
train	treno	*'treno*
train car	vagone	*va'gone*

Could you tell me where ...
Dov'è ...

    ... the information bureau is?
    ... l'ufficio informazioni?
    ... the ticket office is?
    ... la biglietteria?
    ... platform number ... is?
    ... il binario numero ... ?
    ... the bar/refreshment kiosk is?
    ... il bar/ristoro?
    ... the waiting room is?
    ... la sala d'attesa?
    ... the left luggage office is?
    ... il deposito bagagli?
    ... I can find a luggage trolley?/I can find a porter?
    ... un carrello portabagagli?/un facchino?

What is the charge per piece?
Qual è la tariffa per collo?

Please take this luggage ...
Porti il bagaglio ...

    ... to platform ... .
    ... al marciapiede/binario ... .

... **to coach ... .**
... alla carrozza ... .
... to the left luggage office.
... al deposito bagagli.
... to the taxi rank.
... al taxi.

What time is the next train for ... due to leave?
A che ora parte il prossimo treno per ... ?

I'd like information about ...
Vorrei sapere ...

... departures/arrivals ...
... (1)le partenze/gli arrivi ...
... morning/afternoon/evening/overnight ...
... (3)la mattina/il pomeriggio/la sera/la notte.
... for/from ... .
... (2)per/da ...

What platform does the ... (time) train for ... (place) leave from?
Da che binario parte il treno ... delle ore ... per ... ?

What time does it arrive at ... ?
A che ora arriva a ... ?

Does it stop at ... ?
Ferma a ... ?

Do I need to change?
È necessario cambiare?

How long do I have to wait for a connection?
Dopo quanto c'è la coincidenza?

Is there a supplementary charge?/Are reservations compulsory?
C'è supplemento rapido/prenotazione obbligatoria?

Are there any restrictions?
Ci sono limitazioni?

How much is ...
Quanto costa ...

... a first/second class ticket for ... ?
... un biglietto di prima/seconda classe per ... ?

2.4 ON THE TRAIN

... a return ticket for ... ?
... un biglietto di andata e ritorno per ... ?
... the reservation fee?
... la prenotazione?
... the supplementary charge?
... il supplemento?
... a couchette/a sleeping-car?
... la cuccetta/il vagone letto?

How many days is the ticket valid for?
Per quanti giorni è valido il biglietto?

Are there any reduced fares for ...
Ci sono tariffe ridotte per ...

... schoolchildren/students?
... giovani/studenti?
... senior citizens?
... pensionati?
... children under ... years?
... bambini sotto i ... anni?
... disabled persons/parties?
... disabili/gruppi?

Do you offer circular tour tickets?
Ci sono biglietti chilometrici?

Are there any weekly/monthly season tickets?
Ci sono abbonamenti settimanali/mensili?

A single/return ticket for ... .
Un biglietto di andata/andata e ritorno per ... .

A ticket for ... (place) on ... (date).
Un biglietto per ... in data ... .

I'd like to reserve ...
Vorrei prenotare ...

... a (non) smoker's seat on the ... train on ... (date).
... un posto (non) fumatori sul treno ... del giorno ...
... a couchette on the ... train on ... (date).
... una cuccetta sul treno ... del giorno ... .

... a berth in a sleeping car.
... un posto in vagone-letto.
... a single compartment.
... una cabina singola.
... a double/triple compartment.
... una cabina a due/tre letti.

■ **ANNOUNCEMENTS YOU MAY HEAR OVER THE LOUDSPEAKER**

Il treno ... numero ... delle ... proveniente da ... è in arrivo al binario ...
... train number ... due at ... from ... is arriving at platform ... .
Il treno ... numero ... delle ... per ... è in partenza dal binario ... . Ferma a ... .
... train number ... scheduled to leave at ... for ... is about to depart from platform ... ; stopping at ... .
Il treno ... numero ... delle ... viaggia con un ritardo di ... minuti.
... train number ... , scheduled to arrive at ... , will be delayed ... minutes.
Il treno ... numero ... delle ... partirà dal binario ... anziché dal binario ... .
... train number ... scheduled to leave at ... will leave from platform ... instead of platform ... .
Il treno ... numero ... è stato soppresso causa sciopero/per motivi tecnici.
Owing to strike action/technical reasons, ... train number ... has been cancelled.

ON THE TRAIN

compartment	scompartimento	*skomparti'mento*
conductor	controllore	*kontrol'lore*
guard	capotreno	*kapo'treno*
luggage compartment	bagagliaio	*bagaʎ'ʎajo*

2.4 ON THE TRAIN

Is this the ... (time) train for ... ?
È questo il treno delle ... per ... ?
Excuse me, is this seat free?
Scusi, è libero questo posto?

> **No, è occupato.**
> No, I'm afraid it's occupied.

Where is seat ... in coach ... ?
Dov'è il posto ... della carrozza ... ?
I believe this is my seat. I have a reservation.
Questo è il mio posto. Ho la prenotazione.

> **Biglietti, signori!**
> Tickets, please.

Is there a couchette/a berth in the sleeping car?
C'è una cuccetta/un posto nel vagone-letto?
May I open/close the window?
Posso aprire/chiudere il finestrino?
Can you tell me where the dining car is, please?
Dov'è la carrozza ristorante?
Excuse me, may I pass, please?
Permesso, vorrei passare.
Which station are we at?
A che stazione siamo?
Could you tell me, please, when we arrive at ... ?
Può avvisarmi quando arriviamo a ... ?
Could you wake me at ... , please?
Può svegliarmi alle ... ?
Which platform is the connection for ... at?
A che binario si trova la coincidenza per ... ?
Is this the station of ... ?
È questa la stazione di ... ?

TAXIS

Can you tell me where I can find a taxi, please?
Dove posso trovare un taxi?
What is the radio-taxi telephone number?
Qual è il numero telefonico del radio-taxi?
Could you call me a taxi, please?
Mi può chiamare un taxi?
I'd like to book a taxi for today/tomorrow at ... .
Vorrei prenotare un taxi per oggi/domani alle ore ... .
Are you free?
È libero?

> **No, sono fuori servizio.**
> No, I'm afraid I'm off duty.

How much is the fare to ... ?
Quanto costa la corsa fino a ... ?
Are you going to charge me the long-distance/holiday/ night-time rate?
È in vigore la tariffa extraurbana/festiva/notturna?
Please take me ...
Mi porti ...

> **... to this address/to Hotel ... .**
> ... a questo indirizzo/all'hotel ... .
> **... to the airport/to the station.**
> ... all'aeroporto/alla stazione.
> **... to the hospital.**
> ... all'ospedale.
> **... into the centre.**
> ... in centro.
> **... to ... Street/Square.**
> ... in via/piazza ... .

At the corner, turn right/left.
All'angolo giri a destra/sinistra.
Keep straight on.
Continui diritto.

2.5 USING PUBLIC TRANSPORT

I'm in a great hurry!
Ho molta fretta!
May I open the window?
Posso aprire il finestrino?
Could you go more slowly, please?
Potrebbe andare più piano?
Would you stop here, please.
Si fermi qui.
Can you wait for me here? I'll be back in … minutes.
Mi può aspettare qui? Torno fra … minuti.
How much will that be?
Quanto spendo?

■ TAKING THE BUS, TROLLEY OR TRAM

bus stop	fermata	fer'mata
request bus stop	a richiesta	arri'kjɛsta
compulsory bus stop	obbligatoria	obbiga'tɔrja
circle line	circolare	tʃirko'lare
conductor	controllore	kontrol'lore
deposit	deposito	de'pɔzito
line	linea	'linea
terminus	capolinea	kapo'linea

If you plan on using public transport, we advise you to gather informa-tion on their use, rates and timetables at the reception desk of your hotel, at a tourist information bureau or at the transport company offices.

Have you got a guide to public transport, please?
Ha una cartina della rete dei trasporti?
Which bus will take me to … ?
Quale autobus mi porta a … ?
How often does the … bus run?
Con che frequenza passa il … ?
When do buses start/stop running?
A che ora passa il primo/l'ultimo autobus?

USING PUBLIC TRANSPORT 2.5

Do buses run at night?
Ci sono autobus notturni?
Where can I buy a bus ticket?
Dove si compra il biglietto dell'autobus?

> **Direttamente sull'autobus.**
> On board the bus.
> **Dal tabaccaio o in edicola.**
> At tobacco shops or at news-stands.
> **Ai distributori automatici presso le fermate.**
> From automatic vendors at bus stops.

How much is ...
Quanto costa il biglietto ...
   ... a single one-way ticket?
   ... per una corsa singola?
   ... a multiple/10 trip ticket?
   ... multiplo/da dieci corse?
   ... an hourly/a 90 minute/a two hourly ticket?
   ... da 60/90/120 minuti?
   ... a daily travel card?
   ... giornaliero turistico?
   ... a weekly/monthly ticket?
   ... settimanale/mensile?
Are any reduced/season tickets available ...
Ci sono biglietti ridotti/abbonamenti ...
   ... for children/students/disabled persons/groups?
   ... per giovani/studenti/disabili/gruppi?
I'd like a multiple/hourly ticket.
Vorrei un biglietto da ... corse/minuti.
Where is the stop for number ... in the direction of ... ?
Dov'è la fermata del numero ... in direzione ... ?
Does this bus go to ... Street?
Quest'autobus passa da via ... ?

> **No, deve prendere il ... .**
> No, you need number ... .

2.5 USING PUBLIC TRANSPORT

How many stops are there before ... Street?
Quante fermate ci sono da qui a via ... ?

■ ON THE BUS
Is this ... Street?
È questa via ... ?
Can you tell me when to get off for ... , please?
Devo andare in via ... , quando devo scendere?
Excuse me, I need to get off here.
Permesso, devo scendere!

THE UNDERGROUND

We have taken into consideration a complex underground network with many stations and connections. Always check the train's direction and follow the signs, which are usually well marked.

Can you tell me where there is an underground station, please?
Dov'è una stazione della metropolitana?
Have you got a map of the underground, please?
Ha una cartina della rete della metropolitana?
What line do I take for ... ?
Che linea si prende per andare a ... ?

> **Deve prendere la linea ... in direzione ... fino a ... e lì prendere la linea ... in direzione ... .**
> You must take the ... line in the direction of ... as far as ... and then get the ... line going (to) ... .

What time is the first/last train?
A che ora passa il primo/l'ultimo treno?
Are there any special season tickets for tourists?
Ci sono abbonamenti speciali turistici?
I'd like a daily/weekly/monthly ticket.
Vorrei un biglietto giornaliero/settimanale/mensile.
What platform/level does line ... in the direction of ... leave from?
Da quale marciapiede/livello parte la linea ... in direzione ... ?

....

Excuse me, does this train go to ... ?
Questo treno va a ... ?

> **Deve prendere il treno nella direzione opposta.**
> You have to take the train going the other way.
> **Questo treno non ferma a ... .**
> This train does not stop at ... .

Is the next station ... ?
La prossima stazione è ... ?
How many stops are there before ... ?
Quante fermate mancano a ... ?

SIGNS YOU MAY SEE IN THE UNDERGROUND

> **La stazione di ... è chiusa per lavori.**
> ... station is closed for works.
> **All'arrivo del treno non oltrepassare la linea ... .**
> Do not cross over the ... line if a train is approaching.
> **Vietato attraversare i binari.**
> It is strictly forbidden to cross the track.
> **Conservare il biglietto fino all'uscita.**
> Retain/Keep your ticket until the exit.

TRAVELLING ON BUSES AND COACHES

In this case we have considered the needs of those who use coaches for getting from one place to another or for sightseeing excursions. For phrases relative to actual coach tours, see Situation 5.2.

Can you tell me where ...
Dov'è ...

> **... the bus station is, please?**
> ... la stazione degli autobus?
> **... the information/ticket office is, please?**
> ... l'ufficio informazioni/la biglietteria?

Can you give me the times of coaches for ... , please?
Mi può dare gli orari dei pullman per ... ?

2.5 USING PUBLIC TRANSPORT

Do coaches run at weekends and on public holidays?
Ci sono corse nei giorni festivi?
Is there a coach for … ?
C'è un pullman per … ?
Are there guided sightseeing tours of the city by coach?
Ci sono pullman che fanno la visita guidata della città?
How long does the coach take to get to … ?
Quanto impiega il pullman ad arrivare a … ?
How much does a … ticket … cost?
Quanto costa un biglietto …
    … single/return …
    … andata e ritorno …
    … for an adult/a child …
    … per adulti/per bambini …
    … with/without luggage …
    … con/senza bagaglio per … ?
Is there a reduction for children/students/groups/tourists?
Ci sono sconti per giovani/studenti/gruppi/turisti?
How much does a weekly/monthly ticket cost?
Quanto costa l'abbonamento settimanale/mensile?
I'd like to book … seats on the … bus for … .
Vorrei prenotare … posti sull'autobus delle … per … .
I'd like a front/window/(non)smoker's seat.
Vorrei un posto davanti/al finestrino/(non) fumatori.
Will there be any stops on the journey?
Ci saranno soste durante il tragitto?

■ ON THE COACH
Is this seat free?
È libero questo posto?
Excuse me, will you let me through, please?
Mi scusi, mi fa passare?
Can you stop a moment, please. I feel sick.
Può fermare un attimo? Mi sento male.
What time do we get to … ?
A che ora arriveremo a … ?

DOCUMENTS AND PUBLIC OFFICES 2.6

This section groups the expressions and words relative to public offices with which one may get in touch during the course of a normal trip, their relative services, documents and duties. For phrases regarding the theft of documents and other sorts of inconveniences, see Theft and Muggings, Area 4.2.

ambassador	ambasciatore	*ambaʃʃaˈtore*
certificate	certificato	*tʃertifiˈkato*
consul	console	*ˈkɔnsole*
consulate	consolato	*konsoˈlato*
document	documento	*dokuˈmento*
embassy	ambasciata	*ambaʃˈʃata*
nationality	nazionalità	*nattsjonaliˈta*

Can you tell me where ...
Può dirmi dov'è ...

> **... the British embassy is, please?**
> ... l'ambasciata inglese?
> **... the British consulate is, please?**
> ... il consolato inglese?
> **... the immigration office is, please?**
> ... l'ufficio immigrazione?
> **... the harbour master's office is, please?**
> ... la capitaneria di porto?
> **... the office issuing shooting/fishing licences is, please?**
> ... l'ufficio che rilascia licenze di caccia/di pesca?

My passport needs stamping.
Devo vidimare il passaporto.
My temporary residence permit needs renewing.
Devo rinnovare il permesso di soggiorno.
I need a shooting/fishing licence.
Devo fare la licenza di caccia/di pesca.

> **Prego, porto d'armi e matricola del fucile.**
> Your gun licence and gun registration number, please.

2.6 DOCUMENTS AND PUBLIC OFFICES

What documents do I need?
Di quali documenti ho bisogno?

> **Non è necessaria alcuna formalità.**
> No formality is required.
> **La documentazione è incompleta.**
> A few particulars are lacking from your papers.
> **Prego, mi mostri … .**
> Please show me … .

2.7 HIRING A CAR AND OTHER VEHICLES

■ HIRING A CAR

To indicate, if necessary, parts of the car or of the car mechanics at the moment of hiring, see Breakdowns, 4.1.

Can you tell me where there is a car-hire firm, please?
Dov'è un'agenzia di autonoleggio?
I'd like to hire …
Vorrei noleggiare …

> **… a small/medium-sized/big car.**
> … un'auto piccola/media/grande.
> **… a two/four/five-seater car …**
> … un'auto a due/quattro/cinque posti …
> **… with automatic/manual gears.**
> … con il cambio automatico/manuale.
> **… with air conditioning.**
> … con aria condizionata.
> **… with a boot/luggage rack.**
> … con bagagliaio/porta pacchi.

... a diesel-run vehicle.
... un'auto diesel.
... a station wagon.
... una station wagon.
... a minibus/camper for ... persons.
... un pulmino/camper per ... persone.
... a chauffeur-driven car.
... un'auto con autista.

Non ci sono vetture libere.
I'm afraid all the cars are taken.

What are the ... rates ...
Qual è la tariffa ...
... daily ...
... al giorno?
... weekend ...
... per un fine settimana?
... monthly/weekly ...
... per un mese/per una settimana?
... per kilometre/mile?
... chilometrica/a miglio?
Are there any special rates/offers?
Esistono tariffe/offerte speciali?

Tariffa giornaliera a chilometraggio illimitato.
Daily rates with unlimited mileage.

Is insurance included?
È compresa l'assicurazione?

No, l'assicurazione è a parte.
No, insurance is separate.

Does the insurance cover all risks?
L'assicurazione è integrale?
Does the insurance cover ...
L'assicurazione copre ...

2.7 HIRING A CAR AND OTHER VEHICLES

... the driver?
... il guidatore?
... damage to the vehicle/theft?
... i danni al veicolo/il furto?
What is the maximum sum insurable?
Quali sono i massimali?
(This person) will also be driving.
Guiderà anche ... (questa persona).
What is the age-limit for driving it?
Qual è il limite d'età per guidarla?
Would it be possible ...
È possibile ...

   ... to take it abroad?
   ... recarsi all'estero?
   ... to return the car ...
   ... riconsegnare l'auto ...
   ... on a Sunday(holiday)/at night/to another town?
   ... di giorno festivo/di notte/ in un'altra città?

Vorrei vedere la patente di tutte le persone che guideranno l'auto.
I'd like to see the driving licences of all the people who will be driving the car.

È necessaria la patente internazionale.
An international licence is needed.

Per il noleggio è necessaria una carta di credito.
A credit card is needed to hire a car.

Nel prezzo è compreso il pieno: se non restituisce l'auto con il pieno dovrà pagare la differenza.
A full tank is included in the rates. Failure to return the car on a full tank will entail payment of the difference.

Am I to use super petrol/leadless petrol/diesel fuel?
Devo usare benzina super/senza piombo/gasolio?

HIRING A CAR AND OTHER VEHICLES 2.7

Where are the car papers?
Dove sono i documenti dell'auto?
Can you please explain how ... functions?
Mi può spiegare come funziona ... ?
Where is the tool/first aid kit?
Dov'è la cassetta degli attrezzi/del pronto soccorso?
Excuse me,
Scusi ...

   ... the body work is dented.
   ... la carrozzeria è deformata.
   ... the engine won't start.
   ... il motore non si avvia.
   ... the brakes don't work.
   ... l'auto non frena.
   ... the clutch/accelerator doesn't work properly.
   ... la frizione/l'acceleratore non funziona bene.
   ... the head lamps don't light up.
   ... non si accendono i fari.
   ... the indicators/windscreen wipers don't work.
   ... non funzionano le frecce/i tergicristalli.
   ... the door/the window/the bonnet/the boot doesn't close.
   ... lo sportello/il finestrino/il cofano/il bagagliaio non chiude.
   ... the papers are missing.
   ... mancano i documenti.

■ **HIRING OTHER MEANS OF TRANSPORT**
Where can I hire ...
Dove posso noleggiare ...

   ... a bicycle?
   ... una bicicletta?
   ... a moped?
   ... un motorino?
   ... a motor-cycle?
   ... una moto?

81

2.7 HIRING A CAR AND OTHER VEHICLES

... a boat?
... una barca?
What are the daily rates?
Qual è la tariffa giornaliera?
I'd like to hire ... for ... days.
Vorrei noleggiare ... per ... giorni.

> **Mi lasci un documento come deposito.**
> Please leave me a document on deposit.

Is there a hitch-hiking agency anywhere?
C'è un'agenzia di autostop?

AREA 3. LIVING

T his Area addresses the situations that satisfy everyday needs: sleep and rest, food and drink, currency exchange, the post, the telephone, personal hygiene and religion. We wish to underline that Situation 3.2 (Food and Restaurants) was compiled in extreme detail in order to serve properly as a vocabulary for those who wish to purchase ingredients to cook for themselves as well as those who prefer to eat out (for phrases related to buying staples, see Situation 5.4). We have also deliberately taken into account the difference in the needs of those who prefer full meals to those who limit themselves to quick snacks, dedicating a separate section to the latter, for easy consultation.

3.1
HOTELS

3.2
FOOD AND
RESTAURANTS

3.3
MONEY,
POST OFFICES
AND TELEPHONES

3.4
BEAUTY AND
HYGIENE

3.5
RELIGION

HOTEL RESERVATIONS

bathroom	bagno	'baɲɲo
bed	letto	'lɛtto
bedroom	camera	'kamera
single bedroom	singola	'singola
twin bedroom	doppia	'doppja
double bedroom	matrimoniale	matrimo'njale
b. with three beds	tripla	'tripla
blanket	coperta	ko'pɛrta
boarding house/ small hotel	pensione	pen'sjone
cot	lettino per bambini	let'tino perbam'bini
dining room	sala da pranzo	'sala dap'prandzo
doorman	portiere	por'tjɛre
emergency exit	uscita di sicurezza	uʃ'ʃita disiku'rettsa
heating	riscaldamento	riskalda'mento
hotel	albergo	al'bɛrgo
laundry	lavanderia	lavande'ria
lift	ascensore	aʃʃen'sore
maid	cameriere/a	kame'rjɛre/ kame'rjɛra
manager	direttore	diret'tore
operator/ switchboard	centralino	tʃentra'lino
pillow	cuscino	kuʃ'ʃino
pillow case	federa	'fɛdera
sheet	lenzuolo	len'tswɔlo
shower	doccia	'dottʃa

RESERVING THROUGH THE LOCAL TOURIST INFORMATION BUREAU

Making room reservations upon arrival at the local Tourist Bureau has been thought to be the most likely case. Should you be making your reservation by phone, you may go to the next section; we advise you, in any case, to read the following sequence for your information.

Where can I make a hotel booking?
Dove posso prenotare un albergo?
I want to book a hotel in … .
Vorrei prenotare un albergo a … .
I would like a hotel close to …
Vorrei un albergo vicino …
>   **… the centre of town/the stadium/the ski station.**
>   … al centro/allo stadio/agli impianti sciistici.
>   **… the port/the airport/the station.**
>   … al porto/all'aeroporto/alla stazione.

I would like a single/double room.
Vorrei una camera singola/matrimoniale.
I would like a room with two/three beds.
Vorrei una camera a due/tre letti.
I would like a suite.
Vorrei un appartamento.
I want a cheap/average priced/good/luxury hotel.
Vorrei un albergo economico/medio/buono/di lusso.

>   Per quanti giorni/notti?
>   For how many days/nights?

I shall be staying …
Mi tratterrò …
>   **… from … to … .**
>   … dal … al … .
>   **… only tonight/a few days/a week.**
>   … per stanotte/qualche giorno/per una settimana.

3.1 HOTELS

I would like a room with a bath/a shower/a telephone.
Vorrei una camera con bagno/doccia/telefono.
I would like a room with a television/air conditioning.
Vorrei una camera con televisione/aria condizionata.
I would like a quiet room/a room with a view.
Desidero una camera silenziosa/con vista.
Does the hotel have a garage/a restaurant/a lift/a laundry/a swimming pool?
Nell'albergo c'è il garage/il ristorante/l'ascensore/la lavanderia/la piscina?

> Spiacente, tutti gli alberghi sono al completo.
> I'm sorry, all the hotels are full.

Can you try in the surroundings?
Può cercare nelle vicinanze?
How much is the room per night?
Quanto costa la camera a notte?
How much is the suite per week?
Quanto costa l'appartamento a settimana?
Does it include breakfast?
È compresa la prima colazione?
How much does it cost with dinner, bed and breakfast/all meals?
Quanto costa la mezza pensione/pensione completa?
It's too expensive, could you please look for something else?
È troppo caro, cerchi qualcos'altro.
Yes, book in the name of ... .
Sì, prenoti a nome ... .
I shall arrive at ... .
Arriverò alle ... .

> Deve arrivare entro le ... .
> You must arrive before ... .
> Deve pagare ... di acconto, il resto all'albergo.
> You have to pay ... on account and the balance to the hotel.

Ho bisogno di un documento/della carta di credito.
I need an identity document/credit card.

Can you give me a map?
Può darmi una piantina?

■ RESERVING BY PHONE OR AT THE RECEPTION DESK
Do you have a room for tonight/for tomorrow?
Avete una camera libera per stanotte/per domani?
Do you have a room for a week?
Avete una camera libera per una settimana?

No, siamo al completo.
No, I'm afraid we're full.
Sì, abbiamo una camera.
Yes, we have a room.
Non accettiamo prenotazioni telefoniche. Venga di persona.
I'm afraid we don't accept telephone bookings. You should come in personally.

Is it a room with a bath?
La camera è con bagno?

No, con doccia.
No, with a shower.
No, i bagni sono al piano.
No, the bathrooms are on the same floor.

Can you please give me the exact address of the hotel?
Mi può dare l'indirizzo esatto dell'albergo?
How can I reach the hotel?
Come posso raggiungere l'albergo?

Dove si trova lei adesso?
Where are you now?

3.1 HOTELS

WHEN YOU GET TO YOUR HOTEL

When checking in, we advise you to specify how your reservation was made (travel agency, tourist information bureau, phone) and show confirmation of the reservation and/or the receipt of your deposit.

I have reserved ...
Ho riservato ...

> **... by telephone/through an agency/through the
> tourist information office ...**
> ... per telefono/tramite agenzia/tramite tourist info ...
> **... a room/two rooms/in the name of ... .**
> ... una/due camera/e a nome ... .

Quante notti si trattiene?
How many nights will you be staying?

I am staying ... nights/I don't know yet.
Mi trattengo ... notti/non so ancora.
Is it possible to have an extra room?
È possibile avere una camera in più?
Is it possible to have an extra bed/a cot for the baby?
È possibile avere un letto in più/un letto per il bambino?
Where can I park the car?
Dove posso parcheggiare l'auto?
Can you have the luggage taken to the room?
Può far portare i bagagli in camera?
May I deposit this in the safe?
È possibile depositare questo in cassaforte?
May I have my identity documents back?
Mi può restituire i documenti?
At what time is breakfast/lunch/dinner?
Qual è l'orario della colazione/del pranzo/della cena?
What time do you close at night?
Qual è l'orario di chiusura notturna?

Se l'ingresso è chiuso, suoni il campanello.
If the front door is closed, ring the bell.

I would like to extend my stay by a day/ ... days.
Vorrei prolungare la mia permanenza di ... giorno/i.

■ ROOM SERVICE

My room number is ... .
La mia camera è la numero ... .

Switchboard? ...
Centralino? ...

> **... can you please wake me at ... ?**
> ... Mi può svegliare alle ore ... ?
> **... please don't put any telephone calls through to my room.**
> ... Non mi passi telefonate in camera.
> **... may I have an outside line?**
> ... Posso avere la linea esterna?
> **... can you call the number ... in ... for me?**
> ... Può chiamarmi il numero ... di ... ?

> **Resti in linea.**
> Please hold the line.
> **Riagganci, le passerò io la comunicazione.**
> Put your receiver down. I shall ring you back.
> **Il numero è occupato. Devo riprovare?**
> The number is engaged. Shall I try again?
> **Sta squillando.**
> It's ringing.

Could I have some more clothes hangers?
È possibile avere altri appendiabiti?
Could I have some soap/a towel?
È possibile avere del sapone/un asciugamano?
Could I have some toilet paper?
È possibile avere della carta igienica?

3.1 HOTELS

May I have breakfast/meals in the room?
È possibile avere la colazione/i pasti in camera?
Could I have another pillow/another blanket?
È possibile avere un altro cuscino/un'altra coperta?
Is it possible to turn up/to turn down the heating?
È possibile alzare/abbassare il riscaldamento?
Is it possible to switch on/to switch off air conditioning?
È possibile accendere/spengere l'aria condizionata?
What voltage is the electric current?
Qual è il voltaggio della corrente elettrica?
Room service? Can you please bring ... to room number ... ?
Servizio in camera? Per favore, ... alla camera numero ... .
    ... a bottle of ... /a snack/some sandwiches ...
    ... una bottiglia di ... /uno spuntino/dei sandwich ...
    ... some coffee/some tea/breakfast ...
    ... del caffè /del tè /la prima colazione ...
Just a minute.
Aspetti un momento.
Come in.
Entri.
Put it there please.
Appoggi pure lì.
Please put it on my account.
Lo metta sul mio conto.

....

DURING YOUR STAY

*For phrases and words relative to breakfast, the bar and restaurant, see
the section Food and Restaurants, Area 3.2.*

Where is the dining room/the bar?
Dov'è la sala da pranzo/il bar?

Where is the swimming pool/the laundry?
Dov'è la piscina/la lavanderia?

If anyone is looking for me ...
Se qualcuno mi cerca, ...

    ... I shall be back at ... .
    ... sarò di ritorno per le ore ... .

    ... I am in the bar/restaurant.
    ... sono al bar/ristorante.

    ... I am not in until ... .
    ... non ci sono per nessuno fino alle ore ... .

If Mr. ... should look for me, please give him this message.
Se mi cerca il sig. ... , gli dia questo messaggio.

Are there any messages for me?
Ci sono messaggi per me?

I would like to change ... dollars/euro.
Vorrei cambiare ... dollari/euro.

Can you prepare a packed lunch for me?
Mi può far preparare il cestino per il pranzo?

Does the hotel have a bus/taxi service?
L'albergo ha un servizio di pullman/taxi?

■ **PROBLEMS WITH ROOM OR SERVICE**

There is a mistake, I asked for ...
C'è un errore, avevo chiesto ...

    ... a suite.
    ... un appartamento.

    ... a single room.
    ... una camera singola.

3.1 HOTELS

… a double room/a room with three beds.
… una camera doppia/a tre letti.
I asked for a room with …
Avevo chiesto una camera con …
… a bath/a shower.
… bagno/doccia.
… a cot for a child.
… letto per il bambino.
… a telephone/a frigobar/a television.
… telefono/frigo-bar/televisore.
I would like to change my room.
Vorrei cambiare camera.
The room is too noisy/small.
La camera è troppo rumorosa/piccola.
My room has not been cleaned.
La mia camera non è stata rifatta.

The heating/The air conditioning …
Il riscaldamento/l'aria condizionata …
The tap/The shower/The hot water …
Il rubinetto/la doccia/l'acqua calda …
The telephone/The television/The light …
Il telefono/il televisore/la luce …
The toilet flush/The basin drain/The bath drain …
Lo scarico del gabinetto/del lavandino/della vasca …

… does not work.
… non funziona.
The drawer/The cupboard door does not open/close.
Il cassetto/la porta dell'armadio non si apre/chiude.
The door/The window/The shutter does not open/close.
La porta/la finestra/la tapparella non si apre/chiude.
The bed is too hard/soft.
Il letto è troppo duro/morbido.
The towels/The sheets are dirty.
Gli asciugamani/i lenzuoli sono sporchi.

I have lost the key.
Ho perso la chiave.
I am locked out of my room.
Sono rimasto chiuso fuori dalla mia stanza.
Someone has been into my room.
Qualcuno è entrato nella mia stanza.
I have been robbed inside the hotel.
Sono stato derubato all'interno dell'albergo.
I want to make a report/a complaint.
Voglio sporgere denuncia/reclamo.
I want to speak to the manager.
Vorrei parlare con il direttore.

■ PROBLEMS ON THE PART OF THE HOTEL

Dobbiamo spostarla di camera.
I am afraid that we must change your room.
L'ascensore è fuori servizio.
The lift is out of order.
Il servizio in camera è sospeso fino alle ore … .
Room service is not available until … .
Per questo servizio è previsto un sovrapprezzo.
There is an extra charge for this service.
La direzione non si assume responsabilità per eventuali danni ad oggetti dei clienti.
The management cannot be held responsible for any damage to guests' possessions.

3.1 HOTELS

RESERVING A BED AND BREAKFAST HOTEL

Do you have a list of bed and breakfasts?
Avete un elenco dei Bed and Breakfast?
Do you have a room for tonight?
Avete una camera libera per stanotte?

> Siamo al completo.
> I'm afraid we are full.

Can you suggest another bed and breakfast?
Può indicarmi un altro B&B?
How much does the room cost per night?
Quanto costa la camera a notte?
How do I get there?
Come si raggiunge?
By what time do I have to be in at night?
A che ora è la chiusura della porta d'ingresso?
Breakfast is not very generous.
La colazione non è abbondante.

CAMPING AND HOLIDAY RESORTS

Is there a camping ground/holiday resort in the area?
C'è un campeggio/villaggio turistico nella zona?
Where can I camp?
Dove posso fare campeggio libero?

> Il campeggio libero è vietato in tutta la zona.
> Camping is not allowed in this area.

Do you have a place for tonight/three days/one/two/three weeks/for ...
Avete posto per stanotte/tre giorni/una/due/tre settimana/e per ...

> **... a camper/a caravan?**
> ... un camper/una roulotte?

... a small/medium/large tent?
... una tenda piccola/media/grande?

Do you have a bungalow for this/next/the next two/ three week/s?
Avete un bungalow libero per questa/la prossima/due/tre setti- mana/e?

What is the price per day for ...
Qual è il prezzo giornaliero per ...

    ... an adult/a child?
    ... adulto/bambino?

    ... a motor car/bicycle/camper/a motor bike?
    ... automobile/bicicletta/camper/moto?

    ... one person/a plot/a caravan/a tent?
    ... persona/piazzola/roulotte/tenda?

Does it include the cost of the connections?
Il costo degli allacciamenti è compreso?

I would like two plots close together.
Vorrei due piazzole vicine.

Where are/is the bathrooms/showers/drinking water?
Dove sono/è i bagni/le docce/l'acqua potabile?

Where is the water/gas/electricity connection?
Dov'è l'allacciamento dell'acqua/del gas/elettrico?

Where is the shop/the restaurant/the supermarket?
Dov'è lo spaccio/il ristorante/il supermarket?

(To request information on the resort's recreational activities, see the section Shows and Entertainment. Area 5.3)

By what time must I depart?
Entro che ora devo partire?

3.1 HOTELS

RESERVING IN YOUTH HOSTELS

Is there a youth hostel in the area?
C'è un ostello della gioventù nella zona?
Is there an age limit?
C'è limite (minimo/massimo) di età?
Is there a limit to the number of nights I can stay?
C'è un limite di notti di permanenza?

Ci vuole la tessera.
You need a membership card.

How many beds to a room?
Quanti letti per stanza?

Le stanze/camerate sono a … letti.
The rooms have … beds each.

How much does breakfast/do sheets/does a shower cost?
Quanto costa/ano la colazione/le lenzuola/la doccia?
At what time is the front door locked?
A che ora chiude il portone?
By what time must I confirm/vacate the room/the bed?
Entro che ora bisogna confermare/liberare la camera/il posto-letto?
Can valuables be left with the management?
Si possono lasciare valori in direzione?
Where can I leave my luggage?
Dove posso lasciare i bagagli?

APARTMENTS AND BOARDING HOUSES

I would like a furnished apartment with … beds for … .
Vorrei un appartamento ammobiliato con … posti letto per … .
How much does it cost per week/month?
Quanto costa alla settimana/al mese?
Does the price include …
Nel prezzo sono comprese le spese di …

... electricity/heating/water?
... elettricità/riscaldamento/acqua?
... cleaning when I leave?
... pulizie finali?

Are there ... in the apartment?
Nell'appartamento ci sono ...

... sheets and blankets/towels ...
... lenzuola e coperte/asciugamani?
... crockery and kitchen utensils ...
... piatti e stoviglie?

Does the apartment have ...
L'appartamento ha ...

... a fridge/a deep freeze?
... il frigorifero/congelatore?
... a garage/a garden/a terrace?
... il garage/il giardino/il terrazzo?
... a bathroom/hot water/heating?
... il bagno/l'acqua calda/il riscaldamento?
... a telephone/a television/air conditioning?
... il telefono/il televisore/l'aria condizionata?
... a kitchenette/a dishwasher/a washing machine?
... l'angolo cottura/la lavastoviglie/la lavatrice?

Deve firmare il contratto.
You have to sign the contract.
Deve firmare l'inventario degli oggetti contenuti nel-
l'appartamento.
You will have to sign the inventory of items in the apartment.

In my apartment is missing/broken/doesn't work ... .
Nel mio appartamento manca/è rotto/non funziona ... .
These items on the inventory are missing.
Questi oggetti dell'inventario non ci sono.
There is no bed for the baby.
Manca un letto per il bambino.

3.1 HOTELS

CHECKING OUT: CHECKING AND PAYING YOUR BILL

I am leaving immediately/at … ; can you prepare my bill, please?
Parto subito/alle ore … , mi può preparare il conto?

By what time must I leave the room?
A che ora devo lasciare la camera?

Can you have the luggage brought down, please?
Può far portare giù i bagagli?

When I arrived I was told a different price.
All'arrivo mi ha detto un altro prezzo …

The agency told me that the price was … .
Il prezzo dettomi dall'agenzia è di … .

I have already paid the agency. Here's the voucher.
Ho già pagato alla mia agenzia. Ecco il voucher.

This service is included in the price.
Questo servizio è incluso nel prezzo.

I have already paid … on account.
Ho già lasciato … di acconto.

There must be a mistake in the bill.
Ci deve essere un errore nel conto.

I never used this service.
Non ho mai usato questo servizio.

I was very comfortable.
Mi sono trovato molto bene.

FOOD AND RESTAURANTS 3.2

MEALS

The glossary and the phrases of this situation can be used to order meals in restaurants and such, but can also be of use in the case that you wish to do some shopping and cook for yourselves. To find the words and phrases relative to specific foods and methods of preparation, you need to refer to the various meals (breakfast, etc.) and courses (soups, meats, etc.).

dinner	cena	'tʃena
food	cibo	'tʃibo
to eat	mangiare	man'dʒare
snack	spuntino	spun'tino
lunch	pranzo,	'prandzo
	colazione	kolat'tsjone
breakfast	prima colazione	'prima kolat'tsjone

BREAKFAST

For bread and the like, see the specific entry. See also Sauces and Condiments, Fruit and Dessert.

brioche	brioches	bri'ɔʃ
butter	burro	'burro
cafe au lait	caffelatte	kaffel'latte
cappuccino	cappuccino	kapput'tʃino
cereals	cereali	tʃere'ali
cheeses	formaggi	for'maddʒi
chocolate	cioccolata	tʃokko'lata
coffee	caffè	kaf'fɛ
decaffeinated c.	decaffeinato	dekaffei'nato
cold meats	salumi	sa'lumi
cream	panna	'panna
eggs	uova	'wɔva
soft-boiled eggs	alla coque	alla'kɔk

3.2 FOOD AND RESTAURANTS

fried eggs	al tegamino	*altega'mino*
eggs and bacon	con pancetta	*kompan'tʃetta*
poached eggs	in camicia	*inka'mitʃa*
fried eggs	fritte	*'fritte*
hard-boiled eggs	sode	*'sɔde*
scrambled eggs	strapazzate	*strapat'tsate*
ham	prosciutto	*proʃ'ʃutto*
honey	miele	*'mjɛle*
jam/marmalade	marmellata	*marmel'lata*
juice	succo	*'sukko*
citrus juice	di agrumi	*dia'grumi*
pineapple juice	di ananas	*di'ananas*
fruit juice	di frutta	*di'frutta*
tomato juice	di pomodoro	*dipomo'dɔro*
milk	latte	*'latte*
squash	spremuta	*spre'muta*
orange squash	di arancia	*dia'rantʃa*
lemon squash	di limone	*dili'mone*
grapefruit squash	di pompelmo	*dipom'pelmo*
sugar	zucchero	*'tsukkero*
tea	tè	*tɛ*
yoghurt	yogurt	*'jɔgurt*

I would like to have breakfast.
Vorrei fare colazione.
I would like a cooked breakfast.
Vorrei una colazione completa.
I would like a continental breakfast.
Vorrei una piccola colazione.
May I have a little more … .
Vorrei ancora un po' di … .

CHOOSING A RESTAURANT

This section helps you choose a dining spot for a meal. You should bear in mind that a hot meal can be provided also in places different from a formal restaurant.

bar	bar	*bar*
buffet	buffet	*buf'fɛ*
cafè	caffè	*kaf'fɛ*
fish and chip shop	friggitoria	*friddʒito'ria*
kiosk	chiosco	*'kjɔsko*
pastry shop	pasticceria	*pastittʃe'ria*
pub	birreria	*birre'ria*
sandwich shop	panineria	*panine'ria*
snack bar	tavola calda	*'tavola 'kalda*
take-away	rosticceria	*rostittʃe'ria*
tearoom	sala da tè	*'sala dat'tɛ*
wine bar	vineria	*vine'ria*

Where can I eat something hot?
Dove posso mangiare qualcosa di caldo?
Can you tell me where to find a ... restaurant?
Può indicarmi un ristorante ...
　　... nearby/cheap ...
　　... nelle vicinanze/economico?
　　... typical/vegetarian/late night ...
　　... tipico/vegetariano/aperto fino a tardi?
At what time does it open/close?
A che ora apre/chiude?
Can you reach it on foot?
Si può raggiungere a piedi?
Is it necessary to book?
È necessario prenotare?
Can you write down its name and address for me, please?
Mi può scrivere il nome e l'indirizzo?

3.2 FOOD AND RESTAURANTS

These phrases are for reserving a table by phone or for requesting one directly at the restaurant.

I would like to book a table for ... persons, for ... in the name of ... .
Vorrei prenotare un tavolo per ... persone per le ...
a nome ... .

> **Non prendiamo prenotazioni.**
> We don't take bookings.
> **Spiacente, siamo al completo.**
> I'm sorry but we are full.

Can you recommend another restaurant nearby?
Può consigliarmi un altro ristorante vicino?
I have booked a table in the name of ... .
Ho prenotato un tavolo a nome ... .
Do you have a table for ... persons?
Avete un tavolo per ... persone?

> **C'è da aspettare.**
> You'll have to wait, I'm afraid.
> **Stiamo chiudendo.**
> I'm afraid we're closing.

Is this table free?
È libero questo tavolo?

> **Questo tavolo è prenotato.**
> This table is reserved.

I would like a table ...
Vorrei un tavolo ...
> **... outside/in the (non) smokers' section.**
> ... all'aperto/nel settore (non) fumatori.
> **... lontano dalla/vicino alla finestra.**
> ... away from/close to the window.

Where is the bar/coat stand/toilet?
Dov'è il bar/l'attaccapanni/la toilette?
I am waiting for … others.
Sto aspettando altre … persone.

> **Facciamo solo servizio ai tavoli.**
> We have service only at the tables.
> **Serviamo solo menù completi.**
> We serve only complete/full meals.

AT YOUR TABLE

Phrases and expressions necessary to request that something be replaced or added to your table or place setting, and similar needs.

bottle	bottiglia	*bot'tiʎʎa*
cheese dish	formaggiera	*formad'dʒera*
coffee cup	tazzina	*tat'tsina*
cruets	ampolle	*am'polle*
cup, mug	tazza	*'tattsa*
fork	forchetta	*for'ketta*
glass	bicchiere	*bik'kjɛre*
water glass	da acqua	*da'akkwa*
champagne glass	da spumante	*daspu'mante*
wine glass	da vino	*dav'vino*
jug/carafe	brocca/caraffa	*'brɔkka ka'raffa*
knife	coltello	*kol'tɛllo*
napkin/serviette	tovagliolo	*tovaʎ'ʎɔlo*
plate	piatto	*'pjatto*
salt-cellar	saliera	*sa'ljɛra*
small glass	bicchierino	*bikkje'rino*
small plate	piattino	*pjat'tino*
soup plate	scodella	*sko'dɛlla*
soup tureen	zuppiera	*tsup'pjɛra*
straw	cannuccia	*kan'nuttʃa*
tablespoon	cucchiaio	*kuk'kjajo*

3.2 FOOD AND RESTAURANTS

tablecloth	tovaglia	to'vaʎʎa
teaspoon	cucchiaino	kukkja'ino
toothpicks	stuzzicadenti	stuttsika'dɛnti
tray	vassoio	vas'sojo

We need another place setting.
Manca un coperto.
Could you bring a fork/some cutlery/some more bread?
Può portare una forchetta/le posate/dell'altro pane?
Could you bring an ashtray/something to clean with?
Può portare un posacenere/uno smacchiatore?
Could you bring a highchair for the child?
Può portare un seggiolone per il bambino?
Could you take away these things?
Potrebbe portar via queste cose?
Could you bring another glass/knife?
Può portare un altro bicchiere/coltello?

PLACING YOUR ORDER

For the preparation of dishes, see the following sections: Cooking and Special Diet Requests as well as the sections dedicated to the single courses of a meal.

Waiter/waitress.
Cameriere/a, prego.
Could you bring me the menu/wine list?
Mi può portare il menu/la lista dei vini?

> **Volete mangiare alla carta?**
> Do you want to eat à la carte?

We haven't decided yet.
Un momento, non abbiamo ancora scelto.
I'd like to order.
Vorrei ordinare.

....

What can you recommend?
Che cosa mi consiglia?
What is the dish/menu of the day?
Qual è il piatto/il menu del giorno?
What is your/the local speciality?
Qual è la specialità della casa/locale?
Do you have a vegetarian/tourist/fixed price menu?
Avete un menu vegetariano/turistico/a prezzo fisso?
Do you serve light luncheons/suppers?
Avete piatti unici?
Do you have half/children's portions?
Avete mezze porzioni/porzioni per bambini?
Are vegetables included in the price of the dishes?
I piatti sono serviti con contorno incluso nel prezzo?
Is service and cover charge included?
Il servizio e il coperto sono compresi nel prezzo?

> **È tutto compreso.**
> They're all included.
> **Il servizio non è compreso.**
> Service is not included.

As a first course I shall have ... , as a second ... with ... .
Di primo prendo ... , di secondo ... con contorno di ... .

> **Per questo piatto c'è un po' da aspettare.**
> You will have to wait a little for this dish.
> **Di questo piatto serviamo minimo due porzioni.**
> The ... is for a minimum of two people.
> **L'abbiamo terminato.**
> That is finished, I'm afraid.

We'll order our second courses afterwards.
Il secondo lo ordiniamo dopo.
We are in a hurry, would you be able to serve us immediately?
Abbiamo fretta, può servirci subito?
We've been waiting rather long, could you serve us?
È molto che stiamo aspettando, potrebbe servirci?

FOR THOSE WHO SUFFER FROM COELIAC DISEASE...

aromatic vinegar	aceto aromatico	a'tʃeto aro'matiko
barley	orzo	'ɔrdzo
beer	birra	'birra
biscuits, cookies	biscotti	bis'kɔtti
bran	crusca	'kruska
bread	pane	'pane
bread-crumbs	pan grattato	pangrat'tato
candy fruit	frutta candita	'frutta kan'dita
cereals	cereali	tʃere'ali
cocoa powder	polvere di cacao	'polvere dika'kao
coffee essence	essenza di caffè	es'sɛntsa dikaf'fɛ
cold meats	salumi	sa'lumi
emmer	farro	'farro
flour	farina	fa'rina
** wheat flour**	di frumento	difru'mento
fry, fried	fritti	'fritti
gluten	glutine	'glutine
maize	mais	'mais
malt	malto	'malto
meat/fish with	carne/pesce	'karne/ 'peʃʃe
** bread-crumbs**	impanati	impa'nati
millet	miglio	'miʎʎo
oats	avena	a'vɛna
rice	riso	'riso
rye	segale	'segale
soya	soia	'sɔja
thickeners, emulsifiers, stabilisers	addensanti, emulsionanti, stabilizzatori	adden'santi, emulsjo'nanti, stabilid'dzatori
vegetable (hydrolised) proteins (PPH)	proteine vegetali (idrolizzate)	prote'ine ve'dʒetali idrolid'dzate

vegetables au gratin	verdure gratinate	*verd'dure grati'nate*
wheat	frumento	*fru'mento*
wheat germ	germe di grano	*dʒɛrme di'grano*

I suffer from coeliac disease, which is a gluten intolerance leading to serious digestive problems.
Soffro di celiachia, un'intolleranza al glutine che causa gravi problemi digestivi.

Gluten is a substance contained in some cereals.
Il glutine è una sostanza contenuta in alcuni cereali.

I am not allowed to eat pasta, bread, flour, cereals.
Non posso mangiare pasta, pane, farina, cereali.

Would you please cook the rice separately for me, without adding pasta or the salted pasta water?
Per favore, può cuocermi il riso a parte, senza aggiungervi la pasta né l'acqua di cottura della pasta?

Is it possible to cook this dish without .../with another ingredient instead of ... ?
È possibile preparare questo piatto senza .../con un altro ingrediente al posto di ... ?

Are flour/bread even in small quantities among the ingredients of this dish/sauce?
Nella preparazione di questo piatto/sugo impiegate farina/pane anche in piccole dosi?

Does the soup contain any bread-crumbs/cereals?
Ci sono pezzetti di pane/cereali nella minestra?

I would like a salad with no dressing. Could you bring the olive oil and red wine vinegar to the table for me to add?
Vorrei un'insalata, ma senza condimento. Può portarmi olio d'oliva e aceto di vino rosso a parte?

Do not add any other sauce, please.
Per favore, non ci aggiunga altre salse.

3.2 FOOD AND RESTAURANTS

COOKING

baked	al forno	al'forno
boiled	bollito	bol'lito
boiling	bollente	bol'lɛnte
braised	brasato	bra'zato
casseroled	in casseruola	inkasse'rwɔla
cooking method	cottura	kot'tura
to cook	cuocere	'kwɔtʃere
rare	al sangue	al'sangwe
medium	media	'mɛdja
well done	ben cotto	bɛn'kɔtto
dressed/seasoned	condito	kon'dito
fresh	fresco	'fresko
fried	fritto	'fritto
frozen	surgelato	surdʒe'lato
grilled	alla griglia	alla'griʎʎa
in a bainmarie	a bagnomaria	abbaɲɲoma'ria
in a frying-pan	al tegame/	alte'game/
	in padella	impa'dɛlla
in an oven dish	in teglia	in'teʎʎa
marinated	marinato	mari'nato
on a spit	allo spiedo	allos'pjɛdo
pie/pastry	pasticcio	pas'tittʃo
plain	al naturale	alnatu'rale
purée	purea	pu'rɛa
raw	crudo	'krudo
roasted	arrosto	ar'rɔsto
smoked	affumicato	affumi'kato
steamed	al vapore	alva'pore
stew/stewed	stufato/	stu'fato/
	in umido	i'numido
stuffed, filled	farcito, ripieno	far'tʃito ri'pjɛno
warmed-up	al piatto	al'pjatto

How is this dish cooked?
Come è cucinato questo piatto?
What is in this dish?
Quali sono gli ingredienti di questo piatto?
Is it piquant?
È piccante?
I cannot eat … .
Non posso mangiare il … .
Well cooked, please.
Ben cotto, per favore.

■ SPECIAL DIET REQUESTS
Does this contain …
Questo piatto contiene …
  … alcohol/pork/flour/cheese?
  … alcool/carne di maiale/farina/formaggio?
  … fat/fish/salt/egg/sugar?
  … grasso/pesce/sale/uovo/zucchero?
Do you have a diabetic …
Avete … per diabetici?
  … dessert/sweet/menu/sweetener?
  … dessert/dolci/un menu/dolcificante …
Could I have an artificial sweetener?
Potrei avere un dolcificante dietetico?

3.2 FOOD AND RESTAURANTS

SAUCES, BREADS AND CONDIMENTS

bread	pane	'pane
white bread	bianco	'bjanko
brown bread	integrale	inte'grale
toasted bread	tostato	tos'tato
bread rolls	panini	pa'nini
bread sticks	grissini	gris'sini
butter	burro	'burro
crackers	crackers	'krɛker
lemon	limone	li'mone
margarine	margarina	marga'rina
mayonnaise	maionese	majo'nese
mustard	senape	'sɛnape
oil	olio	'ɔljo
corn oil	di mais	di'mais
peanut oil	di arachide	dia'rakide
sunflower seed oil	di girasole	didʒira'sole
olive oil	d'oliva	do'liva
pepper	pepe	'pepe
salt	sale	'sale
sauce	salsa	'salsa
tomato sauce	di pomodoro	dipomo'dɔro
soya sauce	di soia	di'sɔja
tartar sauce	tartara	'tartara
unleavened	azzimo	'addzimo
vinegar	aceto	a'tʃeto

Is it already seasoned?
È già condito?
I would like some vegetables/salad without any dressing.
Vorrei della verdura/dell'insalata senza condimento.

DRINKS

drinks	bevande	be'vande
diet drinks	bevande dietetiche	be'vande dje'tɛtike
can	lattina	lat'tina
beer	birra	'birra
draught beer	alla spina	allas'pina
small beer	piccola	'pikkola
medium beer	media	'mɛdja
large beer	grande	'grande
beer in a can	in lattina	inlat'tina
bottled beer	in bottiglia	imbot'tiʎʎa
light beer	chiara	'kjara
dark beer	rossa	'rossa
dark beer/stout	scura	'skura
cider	sidro	'sidro
lemonade	gassosa/	gas'sosa/
	limonata	limo'nata
orange soda	aranciata	aran'tʃata
tonic	acqua tonica	'akkwa 'tɔnika
water	acqua	'akkwa
mineral water	minerale	mine'rale
still mineral water	naturale	natu'rale
sparkling mineral water	gassata	gas'sata
wine	vino	'vino
house wine	della casa	della'kasa
local wine	del posto	del'posto
estate wine/ choice wine	di marca	di'marka
bottled wine	in bottiglia	imbot'tiʎʎa
carafe of wine	in caraffa	inka'raffa
wine from the barrel	sfuso	'sfuzo

3.2 FOOD AND RESTAURANTS

white wine	bianco	*'bjanko*
rosé wine	rosé	*ro'ze*
red wine	rosso	*'rosso*
dessert wine	da dessert	*daddes'sɛr*
sweet wine	amabile	*a'mabile*
dry wine	secco	*'sekko*
sparkling wine	spumante	*spu'mante*
wine at room	a temperatura	*attempera'tura*
temperature	ambiente	*am'bjɛnte*
chilled wine	di cantina	*dikan'tina*
wine on ice	ghiacciato	*gjat'tʃato*

Cosa ordina da bere?
What would you like to drink?

Could you bring me the wine list?
Può portare la lista dei vini?
Do you serve wine by the glass?
Servite vino in bicchieri?
A carafe of … .
Una caraffa di … .

Abbiamo solo vino in bottiglia.
We have only bottled wine.

A bottle of … .
Una bottiglia di … .
Which are the local wines?
Quali sono i vini della zona?
What is the house wine like?
Com'è il vino della casa?
Can you recommend a wine to go with this dish?
Mi può consigliare un vino per questo piatto?
I would like a beer.
Vorrei una birra.
What brands of beer do you have?
Quali marche di birra avete?

Abbiamo solo birre alla spina/in bottiglia.
We have only draught beer/beer in bottles.

A glass/a glass/a can of … .
Un bicchiere/una coppa/una lattina di … .
May I have a straw?
Potrei avere una cannuccia?

FULL MEALS

■ APÉRITIFS AND STARTERS

For more words relative to Apéritifs, see also Drinks and Liqueurs, while for Starters you may also refer to the vocabulary of Breakfast, Salads and Snacks.

apéritif	aperitivo	aperi'tivo
alcoholic	alcolico	al'kɔliko
light	leggero	led'dʒɛro
dry	secco	'sekko
neat/straight	liscio	'liʃʃo
non-alcoholic	analcolico	anal'kɔliko
of the house	della casa	della'kasa
hors d'oeuvre	antipasti	anti'pasti
hot h. d'o.	caldi	'kaldi
cold h. d'o.	freddi	'freddi
mixed h.d'o.	misti	'misti
anchovies	acciughe	at'tʃuge
asparagus	asparagi	as'paradʒi
avocado	avocado	avo'kado
bacon	pancetta	pan'tʃetta
smoked bacon	affumicata	affumi'kata
canapés	crostini/	kros'tini/
	tartine	tar'tine
caviar	caviale	ka'vjale
clams	vongole	'vongole
crab	granchio	'grankjo

3.2 FOOD AND RESTAURANTS

cucumber	cetriolo	tʃetri'ɔlo
eggs	uova	'wɔva
globe artichokes	carciofi	kar'tʃɔfi
ham	prosciutto	proʃ'ʃutto
smoked ham	affumicato	affumi'kato
cooked ham	cotto	'kɔtto
raw ham	crudo	'krudo
baked ham	di Praga	di'praga
herring	aringhe	a'ringe
lobster/crayfish	aragosta	ara'gɔsta
mackerel	sgombri	'zgombri
smoked m.	affumicati	affumi'kati
melon	melone	me'lone
mushrooms	funghi	'fungi
mussels	cozze	'kɔttse
olives	olive	o'live
oysters	ostriche	'ɔstrike
pâté	paté	pa'te
peppers	peperoni	pepe'roni
pickled tongue	lingua	'lingwa salmis'trata
pickles	sottaceti	sotta'tʃeti
prawns	scampi	'skampi
radishes	ravanelli	rava'nɛlli
Russian salad	insalata russa	insa'lata 'russa
salami	salame	sa'lame
salmon	salmone	sal'mone
sardines	sardine	sar'dine
sausage	salsiccia	sal'sittʃa
seafood salad	insalata di mare	insa'lata di'mare
shrimps	gamberetti	gambe'retti
snails	chiocciole	'kjɔttʃole
truffles	tartufi	tar'tufi
tuna	tonno	'tonno
vegetables in oil	sottoli	sot'tɔli

Could you bring us an apéritif?
Potrebbe servirci un aperitivo?
Is there a buffet of hors d'oeuvres/starters?
C'è un tavolo degli antipasti?
Please bring a selection of starters.
Porti degli antipasti assortiti.
Do you have a wine that will go with the starters?
Avete un vino da antipasti?

■ SALADS

See also the entry on Sauces and Condiments. In Italy salads are served as side dishes and not as starters; therefore, we suggest you specify if you wish to order a salad as an opening to your meal.

salad	insalata	insaˈlata
plain salad	al naturale	alnatuˈrale
green salad	verde	ˈverde
mixed salad	mista	ˈmista
tomato salad	di pomodori	dipomoˈdɔri
rice salad	di riso	diˈriso
salad Niçoise	nizzarda	nitˈtsarda
salad dressed	insalata condita	insaˈlata konˈdita
with oil	con olio	koˈnɔljo
and vinegar	e aceto	eaˈtʃeto
with cream	con panna	komˈpanna
with mustard	con senape	konˈsɛnape

I would like a green/mixed salad with an Italian dressing.
Vorrei un'insalata verde/mista condita con olio e aceto.
Do you have a main course of salad?
Avete piatti unici a base d'insalata?

■ FIRST COURSES (SOUPS AND PASTA DISHES)

broth, consommé	brodo/consommé	brɔdo/konsom'me
with noodles	con pastina	kompas'tina
beef broth/cons.	di manzo	di'mandzo
chicken broth	di pollo	di'pollo
fish soup	di pesce	di'peʃʃe
game soup/broth	di selvaggina	diselvad'dʒina
turtle soup	di tartaruga	ditarta'ruga
vegetable broth	vegetale	vedʒe'tale
cream soup	crema	'krɛma
of asparagus	di asparagi	dias'paradʒi
of mushroom	di funghi	di'fungi
of pea	di piselli	dipi'sɛlli
of leek	di porri	di'pɔrri
soup	minestra/zuppa	mi'nɛstra/'tsuppa
cabbage soup	di cavolo	di'kavolo
crab soup	di granchi	di'granki
fish soup	di pesce	di'peʃʃe
onion soup	di cipolle	ditʃi'polle
potato soup	di patate	dipa'tate
tomato soup	di pomodori	dipomo'dɔri
vegetable soup	di verdure	diver'dure
purée	passato	pas'sato
celery purée	di sedano	di'sɛdano
spinach purée	di spinaci	dispi'natʃi
vegetable purée	di verdure	diver'dure
macaroni	maccheroni	makke'roni
pasta	pastasciutta	pastaʃ'ʃutta
pasta with meat sauce	alla bolognese	allaboloɲ'ɲese
pasta with butter	al burro	al'burro
pasta with tomato sauce	alla salsa di pomodoro	alla'salsa dipomo'dɔro
rice	riso	'riso
buttered rice	al burro	al'burro

curried rice	al curry	al'kɛrri
rice with olive oil	all'olio d'oliva	al'lɔljo doliva
rice in broth	in brodo	im'brɔdo
spaghetti	spaghetti	spa'getti

What is the soup of the day?
Qual è la minestra del giorno?
I would like a thin soup.
Vorrei del brodo magro.
Do you serve rice as a side dish?
Servite il riso di contorno?

■ SIDE DISHES AND HERBS

vegetables	verdure	ver'dure
grilled vegetables	alla griglia	alla'griʎʎa
steamed v.	al vapore	alva'pore
casseroled v.	in casseruola	inkasse'rwɔla
roasted v.	in forno	in'forno
fried v.	in padella	impa'dɛlla
vegetables	verdure	ver'dure
seasoned	condite	kon'dite
with cream	con panna	kom'panna
with oil	con olio	ko'nɔljo
and lemon	e limone	elli'mone
artichokes	carciofi	kar'tʃɔfi
asparagus	asparagi	as'paradʒi
beetroot	barbabietole	barba'bjɛtole
broad beans	fave	'fave
cabbage	cavolo	'kavolo
carrots	carote	ka'rɔte
cauliflower	cavolfiore	kavol'fjore
celery	sedano	'sɛdano
chick-peas	ceci	'tʃetʃi
chicory	cicoria	tʃi'kɔrja
courgettes	zucchini	tsuk'kini
cucumbers	cetrioli	tʃetri'ɔli

117

eggplant/ aubergines	melanzane	melan'dzane
endive	indivia	in'divja
fennel	finocchi	fi'nɔkki
French beans	fagiolini	fadʒo'lini
haricot beans	fagioli	fa'dʒɔli
horseradish	rafano	'rafano
leeks	porri	'pɔrri
lentils	lenticchie	len'tikkje
lettuce	lattuga	lat'tuga
lettuce/salad	insalata	insa'lata
mushrooms	funghi	'fungi
onion	cipolle	tʃi'polle
peas	piselli	pi'sɛlli
peppers	peperoni	pepe'roni
potatoes	patate	pa'tate
chips, fried	fritte	'fritte
matchstick	a bastoncino	abbaston'tʃino
baked	in forno	in'forno
pumpkin	zucca	'tsukka
purée	purè	pu'rɛ
radicchio, chicory	radicchio	ra'dikkjo
radishes	ravanelli	rava'nɛlli
sweetcorn	granturco/mais	gran'turko/'mais
tomatoes	pomodori	pomo'dɔri
turnips	rape	'rape
watercress	crescione	kreʃ'ʃone
basil	basilico	ba'ziliko
bay leaf	alloro	al'lɔro
capers	capperi	'kapperi
chili pepper	peperoncino	peperon'tʃino
garlic	aglio	'aʎʎo
mint	menta	'menta
paprika	paprika	'paprika
parsley	prezzemolo	pret'tsemolo

rosemary	rosmarino	*rozma'rino*
saffron	zafferano	*dzaffe'rano*
sage	salvia	*'salvja*

■ SECOND COURSES

meat	carni	*'karni*
white meat	bianche	*'bjanke*
red meat	rosse	*'rosse*
beef	manzo	*'mandzo*
capon	cappone	*kap'pone*
chicken	pollo	*'pollo*
wing	ala	*'ala*
leg	anca	*'anka*
thigh	coscia	*'kɔʃʃa*
breast	petto	*'pɛtto*
duck	anatra	*'anatra*
game	selvaggina	*selvad'dʒina*
goose	oca	*'ɔka*
guinea-fowl	faraona	*fara'ona*
hare	lepre ·	*'lɛpre*
hen	gallina	*gal'lina*
kid/goat	capretto	*ka'pretto*
lamb	agnello	*aɲ'ɲɛllo*
mutton	castrato	*kas'trato*
pheasant	fagiano	*fa'dʒano*
pigeon	piccione	*pit'tʃone*
pork	maiale	*ma'jale*
poultry	pollame	*pol'lame*
quail	quaglia	*'kwaʎʎa*
rabbit	coniglio	*ko'niʎʎo*
sucking-pig	porcellino	*portʃel'lino*
turkey	tacchino	*tak'kino*
veal	vitello/a	*vi'tɛllo/vi'tɛlla*
venison	capriolo/cervo	*kapri'ɔlo/'tʃɛrvo*
wild boar	cinghiale	*tʃin'gjale*

Pieces

giblets/offal	frattaglie	frat'taʎʎe
head	testina	tes'tina
heart	cuore	'kwɔre
kidney	rognone	roɲ'ɲone
liver	fegato	'fegato
loin	lombata	lom'bata
shin	stinchi	'stinki
shoulder	spalla	'spalla
sweetbreads	animelle	ani'mɛlle
tongue	lingua	'lingwa
tripe	trippa	'trippa
trotters	zampa/zampetti	'tsampa/tsam'petti

Cuts

chop	braciola	bra'tʃɔla
cutlet/chop	cotoletta	koto'letta
entrecôte	costata	kos'tata
escalope	scaloppina	skalop'pina
fillet	filetto	fi'letto
roast beef	rosbif	'rɔzbif
steak	bistecca	bis'tekka

Ways of serving meat

black pudding	sanguinaccio	sangwi'nattʃo
gelatine	gelatina	dʒela'tina
meat balls	polpette	pol'pette
minced/ground	macinata	matʃi'nata
patty	svizzera	'zvittsera
rolled and filled	involtini	invol'tini
rounds	medaglioni	medaʎ'ʎoni
stew	spezzatino	spettsa'tino
with bacon	lardellato	lardel'lato

FOOD AND RESTAURANTS 3.2

Do you have some cold meats?
Avete un piatto freddo di carne?
I would like a roast pork shin.
Vorrei uno stinco di maiale al forno.
I would like a veal escalope.
Vorrei una scaloppina di vitello.
I would like a grilled entrecôte, well done.
Vorrei una costata di manzo ai ferri ben cotta.

■ FISH

fish	pesce	'peʃʃe
baked fish	al forno	al'forno
blue fish	azzurro	ad'dzurro
boiled fish	lesso	'lesso
fried fish	frittura	frit'tura
grilled fish	alla griglia	alla'griʎʎa
white fish	bianco	'bjanko
slice/steak	trancio	'trantʃo
anchovies	acciughe	at'tʃuge
angler/frog fish	rana pescatrice	'rana peska'tritʃe
bass	branzino	bran'dzino
carp	carpa	'karpa
cod	merluzzo	mer'luttso
crab	granchio	'grankjo
cuttlefish	seppie	'seppje
dentex/bream	dentice	'dɛntitʃe
eel	anguilla	an'gwilla
fluke	platessa	pla'tessa
gilt-head	orata	o'rata
grey mullet	muggine	'muddʒine
hake	nasello	na'sɛllo
John Dory	pesce San Pietro	'peʃʃe sam'pjɛtro
lobster	aragosta	ara'gɔsta
mackerel	sgombro	'zgombro
mussels	cozze	'kɔttse

octopus	polpo	''polpo
perch	persico	'pɛrsiko
pike	luccio	'luttʃo
prawns	gamberi/scampi	'gamberi/'skampi
red mullet	triglia	'triʎʎa
salmon	salmone	sal'mone
sardines	sardine	sar'dine
scallops	capesante/	kape'sante/
	pettini	'pɛttini
scorpion fish	pesce cappone/	'peʃʃe kap'pone/
	scorfano	'skɔrfano
seafood	frutti di mare	'frutti di'mare
shellfish	molluschi	mol'luski
shrimp	gamberetti	gambe'retti
sole	sogliola	'sɔʎʎola
squid	calamari	kala'mari
stockfish	stoccafisso	stokka'fisso
sturgeon	storione	sto'rjone
swordfish	pescespada	peʃʃes'pada
trout	trota	'trɔta
tuna/tunny	tonno	'tonno
turbot	rombo	'rombo
whitebait	bianchetti	bjan'ketti

■ OMELETTES, PIES AND PIZZA
For the preparation of eggs, see above: Breakfast.

omelette	frittata	frit'tata
sweet omelette	dolce	'doltʃe
savoury omelette	salata	sa'lata
ham omelette	al prosciutto	alproʃ'ʃutto
cheese omelette	al formaggio	alfor'maddʒo
spinach omelette	agli spinaci	aʎʎispi'natʃi
vegetable omelette	alle verdure	allever'dure
pizza	pizza	'pittsa
pie	tortino	tor'tino

■ **CHEESE**

cheese	formaggio	for'maddʒo
cow's milk ch.	bovino	bo'vino
sheep's milk ch.	ovino	o'vino
fresh cheese	fresco	'fresko
crumbly cheese	friabile	fri'abile
melted cheese	fuso	'fuzo
high-fat cheese	grasso	'grasso
low-fat cheese	magro	'magro
ripe cheese	maturo	ma'turo
piquant cheese	piccante	pik'kante
mature cheese	stagionato	stadʒo'nato

■ **FRUIT**

fruit	frutta	'frutta
seasonable fruit	di stagione	dista'dʒone
fresh fruit	fresca	'freska
cooked/stewed f.	cotta	'kɔtta
mixed fruit	mista	'mista
dried fruit	secca	'sekka
fruit jelly	gelatina di frutta	dʒela'tina di'frutta
fruit salad	macedonia	matʃe'dɔnja
almond	mandorla	'mandorla
apple	mela	'mela
apricot	albicocca	albi'kɔkka
banana	banana	ba'nana
blackberry/ mulberry	more	'mɔre
blueberries	mirtilli	mir'tilli
cherry	ciliegia	tʃi'ljedʒa
chestnut	castagna	kas'taɲɲa
coconut	noce di cocco	'notʃe di'kɔkko
gooseberry	uvaspina	uvas'pina
grape	uva	'uva
grapefruit	pompelmo	pom'pɛlmo

3.2 FOOD AND RESTAURANTS

hazelnuts	nocciole	not'tʃɔle
kiwi	kiwi	'kiwi
lemon	limone	li'mone
mandarin	mandarino	manda'rino
melon	melone	me'lone
nectarine	pesca-noce	pɛska'notʃe
orange	arancia	a'rantʃa
peach	pesca	'pɛska
peanuts	noccioline	nottʃo'line
pear	pera	'pera
pineapple	ananas	'ananas
plum	susina	su'sina
prunes	prugne	'pruɲɲe
quince	mela cotogna	'mela ko'toɲɲa
raisins	uva passa	'uva 'passa
raspberry	lampone	lam'pone
red and	ribes rosso	'ribes 'rosso
black currant	e nero	e'nero
strawberry	fragola	'fragola
sweet orange	melarancia	mela'rantʃa
walnuts	noci	'notʃi
watermelon	anguria	an'gurja

■ DESSERT

custard	crema	'krɛma
creme chantilly	chantilly	ʃantil'li
confectioners' cream	pasticcera	pastit'tʃɛra
dessert	dolce	'doltʃe
fritters	frittelle	frit'tɛlle
ice cream	gelato	dʒe'lato
mousse	mousse	mus
pastries/teacakes	pasticcini	pastit'tʃini
pudding	budino	bu'dino
tart	torta	'torta

124

fruit tart	di frutta	di'frutta
apple tart	di mele	di'mele
whipped cream	panna montata	'panna mon'tata

Do you have your own dessert specialty?
Avete un dolce della casa?
Could you bring me the dessert trolley?
Può portarci il carrello dei dolci?
Is this dessert made by yourselves?
Questo dolce è fatto in casa?
What is this made with?
Con cosa è preparato?

■ LIQUEURS AND COFFEE

brandy	brandy	'brɛndi
cocktail	cocktail	'kɔkteil
light cocktail	leggero	led'dʒɛro
dry cocktail	secco	'sekko
cognac	cognac	koɲ'ɲak
schnaps	grappa/acquavite	'grappa/akkwa'vite
vermouth	vermut	'vɛrmut
whisky	whisky	'wiski
w. with water	con acqua	ko'nakkwa
w. with ice	con ghiaccio	kon'gjattʃo
w. with soda	con soda	kon'sɔda
neat/straight w.	liscio	'liʃʃo

Do you have liqueurs?
Avete liquori?
A double … , please.
Per favore, un … doppio.
I would like an espresso coffee.
Vorrei un caffè.

3.2 FOOD AND RESTAURANTS

SNACKS

These words and phrases are useful when stopping for a quick bite to eat between museum visits and sightseeing, instead of dining at a formal restaurant. For more complete vocabulary, see Drinks, Sauces and Condiments, Salads, Cheese, Eggs and Breakfast.

a sandwich	tramezzino	tramed'dzino
a toasted sandwich	toast	tɔst
filled bread roll	panino imbottito	pa'nino imbot'tito
slice	fetta	'fetta
snack	spuntino	spun'tino

Where can I have a snack?
Dove posso fare uno spuntino?
I would like a hot-dog/hamburger.
Vorrei un hot-dog/hamburger.
I would like a bread roll with … .
Vorrei un panino con … .
I would like a slice/portion/piece of … .
Vorrei una fetta/porzione/un pezzo di … .
I would like a mixed salad.
Vorrei un'insalata mista.
What is this?
Che cos'è questo?
Can you point to the ingredients on this list?
Può indicarmi gli ingredienti su questa lista?
Is it piquant?
È piccante?
Do you serve hot dishes?
Servite piatti caldi?
Could you bring me a napkin?
Mi può dare un tovagliolino?
Could you bring me some cutlery and a bread roll?
Vorrei le posate e un panino.

FOOD AND RESTAURANTS 3.2

CHANGING YOUR ORDER, COMPLIMENTS AND COMPLAINTS

bad/off	guasto	'gwasto
burnt	bruciato	bru'tʃato
burnt/overcooked	scotto	'skɔtto
complaint	reclamo	re'klamo
foul smelling	puzzolente	puttso'lɛnte
greasy	unto	'unto
hard/tough/stale	duro	'duro
heavy	indigesto	indi'dʒɛsto
salted/salty	salato	sa'lato
sour	acido	'atʃido
sour/tart	aspro	'aspro
stale	raffermo	raf'fermo
tasteless	insipido	in'sipido

Could I change my order?
Potrei cambiare l'ordinazione?
I ordered ... , not this.
Ho ordinato del ... , non questo.
You have forgotten to bring ... .
Ha dimenticato di portare ... .
May I have some more ... ?
Potrei avere ancora del ... ?
Your portions are rather small.
Le vostre porzioni sono troppo piccole.
I ordered a half-portion.
Avevo chiesto mezza porzione, non una intera.
This ... has a rather strange taste/smell.
Questo piatto ha uno strano sapore/odore.
I think this food is off.
Questo cibo è guasto.
The soup is cold.
La minestra è fredda.

The pasta is burnt/overcooked.
La pasta è scotta.
The meat is tough/off.
La carne è dura/puzza.
The salad is not properly washed.
L'insalata non è ben lavata.
The bread is stale.
Il pane è raffermo.
Will you call the manager/owner for me?
Mi chiami il direttore/il proprietario.

> È di suo gradimento?
> Is it alright for you?

This ... is very good.
Questo piatto è ottimo.
Compliments to the chef.
Complimenti allo chef.

CHECKING AND PAYING THE BILL

In Italy, restaurants charge a small fee called the "coperto" per person; this charge covers the place setting, bread, condiments (oil and vinegar) and service. Nevertheless, as with the rest of the world, it is habit to reward the good service of a waiter with a tip. It is also becoming quite common to pay restaurant bills with credit cards and to fill in the amount you wish to leave for a tip in the relative box on the credit card charge slip. To simplify matters, we would advise you to simply give your tip to the waiter in cash. Also, the waiter may ask each person in your party what they ordered, so as to draw up separate bills.

Will you bring me the bill, please?
Mi porta il conto?

> **Conti separati?**
> Do you want separate bills?

All together.
Tutto insieme.
What is this amount for?
Che cos'è questa cifra?
Is cover charge and service included?
Il servizio e il coperto sono compresi?

> **È tutto compreso.**
> It's all included.

May I pay by credit card/travellers' cheque?
Posso pagare con carta di credito/traveller's cheques?
I think there is a mistake here.
Credo che ci sia un errore.
I didn't order this.
Non ho ordinato questo.
Please call the manager.
Chiami il direttore.

> **Paghi alla cassa.**
> Please pay at the cashier.

3.3 MONEY, POST OFFICES AND TELEPHONES

ASKING PRICES AND PAYING

How much does it cost?
Quanto costa?
Can you write down the price for me?
Mi può scrivere il prezzo (la cifra)?
Do I have to pay in cash?
Devo pagare in contanti?
Do you accept credit cards?
Accetta la carta di credito?
Do you accept traveller's cheques?
Accetta travellers' cheques?
May I pay in British pounds?
Posso pagare in sterline?
What is the exchange rate?
Qual è il cambio?
Can you please change this note for me?
Mi può cambiare questa banconota in monete?
It's rather expensive.
È un po' caro.
Do you have something cheaper?
Ha qualcosa di più economico?
Can you give me any discount?
Mi può fare un po' di sconto?
Could you give me an invoice?
Può fare fattura?
May I have a receipt?
Posso avere la ricevuta/lo scontrino?

BANKS AND CURRENCY EXCHANGE

We remind you that for nearly all bank transactions, personal identification is required.

agency	agenzia	adʒen'tsia
bank	banca	'banka
cashier	cassa	'kassa
counter	sportello	spor'tɛllo
foreign currency	valuta	va'luta
form	modulo	'mɔdulo

Where is the nearest bank?
Dov'è la banca più vicina?
Where is an exchange office/automatic banking machine?
Dov'è un ufficio di cambio/un cambio automatico?
What are banking hours?
Qual è l'orario delle banche?
What is the exchange rate today?
Qual è il cambio di oggi?
How much is the commission?
Quanto è la commissione?
I would like to change ... British pounds into ... euro.
Vorrei cambiare ... sterline in ... euro.
I would like to cash this traveller's cheque.
Vorrei incassare questo travellers' cheque.
I would like to make a cash withdrawal on my credit card.
Vorrei fare un prelievo di ... con la carta di credito.
I would like to make a deposit to account number ... in the name of ... .
Vorrei fare un versamento sul conto numero ... intestato a ... .
I would like ... notes.
Vorrei delle banconote da ... .
I would like ... coins.
Vorrei delle monete da ... .

I am waiting for a money transfer from ... .
Aspetto un bonifico da ... .

To buy stamps, we suggest you fill in the address of your correspondence and show it to the clerk who will calculate the exact amount of postage required. In Italy stamps can be bought at Tobacco Shops (Tabacchi) as well as Post Offices.

Where can I buy stamps?
Dove posso comprare dei francobolli?
Where's the nearest post office?
Dov'è l'ufficio postale più vicino?
What are the post office hours?
Qual è l'orario degli uffici postali?
Is there a fast/express postal service?
Esiste un servizio di posta celere?
I would like stamps for ... to Great Britain.
Vorrei un'affrancatura per ... per la Gran Bretagna.

  ... a postcard/a letter ...
  ... una cartolina/una lettera ...
  ... an airmail letter/an express letter ...
  ... via aerea /un espresso ...

  L'indirizzo non è completo, manca ...
  The address is incomplete; ... is missing.
  ... il mittente.
  ... the sender ...
  ... il codice di avviamento postale.
  ... the postal code ...
  C'è un sovrappeso di ... grammi.
  It is overweight by ... grams.

Where is the posting box?
Dov'è la cassetta delle lettere?

I want to send ...
Vorrei spedire ...

> **... an insured letter/a registered letter.**
> ... un'assicurata/una raccomandata.
> **... a packet/an insured packet.**
> ... un pacco/un pacco raccomandato.
> **... a telegram/a fax/a money order.**
> ... un telegramma/un fax/un vaglia.

> **Deve compilare questo modulo.**
> You must complete this form.

How long will it take?
Quanto tempo impiegherà per arrivare?

> **Deve compilare la dichiarazione doganale.**
> You must complete the customs form.

Where is the poste restante?
Dov'è il fermo posta?
Is there any post for Mr ... ?
C'è posta per il sig. ... ?

PUBLIC TELEPHONES

Here are some useful terms to find and use a public phone and request information on the rates and telephone directories. These words and phrases may also be useful when communicating with a hotel switchboard operator (Sit. 3.1).

call	telefonata	telefo'nata
reverse charges/	a carico del	ak'kariko
collect call	destinatario	deldestina'tarjo
intercontinental c.	intercontinentale	interkontinen'tale
international call	internazionale	internattsjo'nale
long-distance call	interurbana	interur'bana
local call	urbana	ur'bana

operator	centralino	tʃentra'lino
tariff/rate	tariffa	ta'riffa
weekend rate	festiva	fes'tiva
full rate	intera	in'tera
nightime rate	notturna	not'turna
unit	scatto	'skatto

Where is a public telephone?
Dov'è un telefono pubblico?
How does one use this telephone?
Come si usa questo telefono?

> **Deve usare monete da … .**
> You must use a … coin.
> **Deve usare la scheda telefonica/carta di credito.**
> You have to use a phone-card/credit card.

Where can I get a phone-card?
Dove posso acquistare una carta/scheda telefonica?
Can I call Great Britain from this phone?
È possibile chiamare la Gran Bretagna da questo telefono?
What is the dialling code for Great Britain?
Qual è il prefisso per la Gran Bretagna?
How much does a three minute call to Great Britain cost?
Quanto costa una telefonata di tre minuti in Gran Bretagna?
Are there hours when the rate is reduced?
Ci sono fasce orarie a tariffa ridotta?
What is the prefix for … ?
Qual è il prefisso di … ?
What is the number here?
Che numero ha questo apparecchio?
Can I receive calls on this phone?
Posso ricevere telefonate da questo apparecchio?
Do you have a telephone directory/the yellow pages for … ?
Ha l'elenco del telefono/pagine gialle di … ?

To make a direct call or a reverse charges call?
Per effettuare una telefonata diretta o a carico del destinatario?
I would like to call the number ... .
Vorrei chiamare il numero ... .
I would like to make a reverse charges call to Mr ... from ... .
Vorrei chiamare il numero ... a carico del destinatario, da parte
del sig ... .

Può telefonare direttamente da questo apparecchio.
You can dial direct from this telephone.
Può rispondere, le passo la comunicazione.
You can speak now; I'm putting your call through.
La linea è sovraccarica.
The line is busy.
Il numero è occupato.
The number is engaged.
Non risponde.
There is no reply.
Attenda in linea.
Please hold on.

I'm afraid I cannot get a line.
Non riesco a prendere la linea.
Hello, may I speak to Mr ... ?
Pronto, vorrei parlare con il sig ... .

Le passo l'interno.
I will put you through.
L'interno non risponde.
There is no reply from that extension.

Can you ask him to call Mr ... on ... ?
Può dirgli di richiamare il sig. ... al numero ... ?
The telephone is out of order.
Il telefono è guasto.
We were cut off.
È caduta la linea.

■ SENDING A FAX

Where can I send a fax from?
Da dove posso spedire un fax?
I would like to send this fax to the number ... .
Vorrei inviare questo fax al numero ... .

> Il testo è illeggibile.
> The text is illegible.
> Il fax non passa.
> The fax won't go through.

What is the fax number here?
Che numero ha questo fax?
Is there a fax for Mr ... ?
Ci sono fax per il sig ... ?

PERSONAL HYGIENE

basin	lavandino	*lavan'dino*
flush	sciacquone	*ʃak'kwone*
hand towel	salvietta	*sal'vjetta*
hygiene	igiene	*i'dʒɛne*
nailbrush	spazzolino	*spattso'lino*
	da unghie	*da'ungje*
soap	sapone	*sa'pone*
sponge	spugna	*'spuɲɲa*
tap	rubinetto	*rubi'netto*
toothbrush	spazzolino	*spattso'lino*
	da denti	*dad'dɛnti*
toothpaste	dentifricio	*denti'fritʃo*

Where is the bathroom?
Dov'è il bagno?
Where is the toilet?
Dov'è la toilette?

> **La toilette è occupata.**
> The toilet is engaged/occupied.

Can you give me ... please?
Mi può dare ...

> **... some soap/a towel ...**
> ... del sapone/l'asciugamano?
> **... some toilet paper/the bathroom key ...**
> ... la carta igienica/la chiave del bagno?

The bath is dirty.
Il bagno è sporco.

■ HEALTH AND HYGIENE OF NEWBORNS

bib	bavaglino	*bavaʎ'ʎino*
bottle	biberon	*bibe'rɔn*
dummy	succhiotto	*suk'kjɔtto*

3.4 BEAUTY AND HYGIENE

homogenized	omogeneizzato	omodʒeneid'dzato
nappy	pannolino	panno'lino
talcum powder	talco	'talko

COSMETICS AND BEAUTY

bathsalts	sali da bagno	'sali dab'baɲɲo
brush	spazzola	'spattsola
cocoa butter	burro di cacao	'burro dika'kao
cologne	acqua di colonia	'akkwa diko'lɔnja
corn plaster	callifugo	kal'lifugo
cotton wool	cotone idrofilo	ko'tone i'drɔfilo
cream	crema	'krɛma
acne cream	anti acne	anti'akne
day cream	da giorno	dad'dʒorno
night cream	da notte	dan'nɔtte
depilatory cream	depilatoria	depila'tɔrja
moisturiser	idratante	idra'tante
cream for dry/	per pelle secca/	per'pɛlle 'sekka/
oily skin	grassa	'grassa
normal skin	pelle normale	'pɛlle nor'male
face cream	per viso	per'vizo
hand cream	per mani	per'mani
sun cream	solare	so'lare
deodorant	deodorante	deodo'rante
eye-shadow	ombretto	om'bretto
eyebrow pencil	matita per occhi	ma'tita pe'rɔkki
face powder	cipria	'tʃiprja
foundation	fondotinta	fondo'tinta
hot wax depilation	ceretta a caldo	tʃe'retta ak'kaldo
wax depilation	a freddo	af'freddo
lotion	lozione	lot'tsjone
make-up brush	pennello	pen'nɛllo
make-up removal	tamponi	tam'poni
pads	da strucco	das'trukko

make-up remover	latte detergente	'latte deter'dʒɛnte
massage	massaggio	mas'saddʒo
mirror/make-up mirror	specchietto	spek'kjetto
nail file	lima per unghie	'lima pe'rungje
nail polish remover	solvente per unghie	sol'vɛnte pe'rungje
powder puff	piumino per cipria	pju'mino per'tʃiprja
skin tonic	tonico	'tɔniko
sun lamp	lampada abbronzante	'lampada abbron'dzante
sun oil	olio solare	'ɔljo so'lare
tweezers	pinzette	pin'tsette

Where can I find a chemist/the cosmetics department?
Dove si trova una profumeria/il reparto cosmetici?

Where can I find a beauty salon/a sauna?
Dove si trova un salone di bellezza/una sauna?

Where can I find a hydromassage/a steam bath?
Dove si trova un idromassaggio/un bagno turco?

I'd like to make an appointment for … (time) to have … .
Vorrei fissare un appuntamento per le ore … per fare … .

    … a manicure/a pedicure/a facial.
    … la manicure/la pedicure/la pulizia del viso.

    … a make-up session/a depilation.
    … un trucco/una depilazione.

May I try this lipstick/nail polish/perfume?
Posso provare questo rossetto/smalto/profumo?

Can I see what nail polish/lipstick colours you have?
Posso vedere i colori degli smalti/rossetti?

I want a lighter/darker colour.
Vorrei un colore più chiaro/scuro.

Could you put a light make-up on for me?
Mi metta un trucco leggero.

3.4 BEAUTY AND HYGIENE

I would like a lipstick of this colour.
Vorrei un rossetto di questo colore.
This corn is hurting me.
Mi fa male questo callo.
The wax is too hot.
Questa ceretta è troppo calda.
Will I have to wait long?
C'è molto da attendere?

THE HAIRDRESSER, THE BARBER

aftershave	dopobarba	*dopo'barba*
balm	balsamo	*'balsamo*
beard	barba	*'barba*
bleach	decolorazione	*dekolorat'tsjone*
comb	pettine	*'pɛttine*
curlers	bigodini	*bigo'dini*
dandruff	forfora	*'forfora*
friction	frizione	*frit'tsjone*
fringe	frangia	*'frandʒa*
hair	capelli	*ka'pelli*
oily hair	grassi	*'grassi*
normal hair	normali	*nor'mali*
dry hair	secchi	*'sekki*
straight hair	lisci	*'liʃʃi*
wavy hair	mossi	*'mɔssi*
curly hair	ricci	*'rittʃi*
hairstyle	pettinatura	*pettina'tura*
moustache	baffi	*'baffi*
peroxided	ossigenato	*ossidʒe'nato*
razor blade	lametta	*la'metta*
razor	rasoio	*ra'sojo*
safety razor	di sicurezza	*disiku'rettsa*
electric razor	elettrico	*e'lɛttriko*
scissors	forbici	*'fɔrbitʃi*

shave	rasatura	raza'tura
shaving brush	pennello da barba	pen'nɛllo dab'barba
shaving cream	crema da barba	'krɛma dab'barba
shaving foam	schiuma da barba	'skjuma dab'barba
shaving soap	sapone da barba	sa'pone dab'barba
sideburns	basette	ba'zette
styptic	emostatico	emos'tatiko
wig	parrucca	par'rukka

Can you tell me where a hairdresser for women/men is?
Può indicarmi un parrucchiere da donna/uomo?

I would like to make an appointment for … .
Vorrei fissare un appuntamento per … .

At what time can I come back?
A che ora posso ritornare?

I would like a shave/a haircut and shave.
Vorrei radermi/fare barba e capelli.

I would like a set/a perm.
Vorrei fare la messa in piega/la permanente.

I would like a wash and cut/a colour rinse.
Vorrei lavare e tagliare/tingere i capelli.

I would like my beard/hair trimmed.
Vorrei spuntare la barba/i capelli.

> Desidera una lozione?
> Would you like a hair lotion?

I would like my hair …
Vorrei i capelli …

> **… tapered upwards/downwards.**
> … con la sfumatura alta/bassa.
> **… not too short/layered.**
> … non troppo corti/scalati.
> **… a little shorter/longer …**
> … un po' più corti/lunghi …

3.4 BEAUTY AND HYGIENE

... in front/at the back/on the sides/on top.
... davanti/dietro/sui lati/in alto.
Please will you give me a(n) anti-dandruff/normal shampoo?
Mi faccia uno shampoo antiforfora/normale.
Please use a shampoo for greasy hair/dry hair.
Mi faccia uno shampoo per capelli grassi/per capelli secchi.

3.5 RELIGION

PLACES OF WORSHIP AND RELIGIOUS SERVICES

See also Area 5.2, p. 151.

| worship | culto | 'kulto

Where is ...
Dov'è ...
    ... a Catholic church/a Protestant church?
    ... una chiesa cattolica/protestante?
    ... a synagogue/a mosque?
    ... una sinagoga/una moschea?
At what times are the services?
Qual è l'orario delle funzioni?
I would like to speak to a priest.
Vorrei parlare con un sacerdote/con un pastore.
Is there a priest who speaks English?
C'è un sacerdote che parli inglese?
I would like to take communion.
Vorrei comunicarmi.
I would like to take confession.
Vorrei confessarmi.
Who is the patron saint of the city?
Qual è il santo patrono della città?

AREA 4. PROBLEM SOLVING

T his Area, we hope, is destined to be the least used of the phrase book. Nevertheless, it has been organised with great care and detail in order to be of maximum use and easy consultation in situations where there is little time to lose and one might not be in the mood to look up words in the dictionary. Naturally, the phrases of this area are complemented by terms and expressions of other sections of the book (particularly in the case of mechanical breakdown or lost objects): such cases are noted within the body of the phrases. In Situation 4.4 the vocabulary of the section dedicated to The Chemist also contains, for obvious reasons of relevance, names of products that are not necessarily therapeutic but for hygienic use (such as mouth wash or eye drops).

4.1
EMERGENCIES

4.2
THEFT, DAMAGE, ASSAULT

4.3
BEARINGS

4.4
HEALTH

4.1 EMERGENCIES

DANGER AND CALAMITIES

To ask or give help (in person or by phone) in case of illness, accidents (including automobile accidents for which we have dedicated a separate section concerning the relevant civil and penal aspects), or dangerous situations. For more vocabulary relative to trauma or physical injury, see also the following section on Health.

accident	incidente	intʃi'dɛnte
alarm	allarme	al'larme
burn	ustione	us'tjone
casualty	ferito	fe'rito
severe casualty	grave	'grave
slight casualty	leggero	led'dʒero
collision	investimento	investi'mento
corpse	cadavere	ka'davere
crash	urto	'urto
crushing	schiacciamento	skjattʃa'mento
drowning	annegamento	annega'mento
electrical discharge	folgorazione	folgorat'tsjone
explosion	esplosione	esplo'zjone
extinguisher	estintore	estin'tore
fall	caduta	ka'duta
first aid	pronto soccorso	'pronto sok'korso
fracture	frattura	frat'tura
frostbite	congelamento	kondʒela'mento
gas leak	fuga di gas	'fuga di'gas
heart attack	infarto	in'farto
injury	ferita	fe'rita
poisoning	avvelenamento	avvelena'mento
shock	shock	ʃɔk
sting	puntura	pun'tura
suffocation	soffocamento	soffoka'mento
trauma	trauma	'trauma

Help!	Aiuto!	*a'juto*
Fire!	Al fuoco!	*al'fwɔko*
It's urgent!	È urgente!	*ɛur'dʒɛnte*
Watch out!	Attenzione!	*atten'tsjone*

Could you help me, please?
Mi può aiutare?
Is there a telephone here?
C'è un telefono?
What is the ambulance/the police/the fire brigade telephone number?
Qual è il numero dell'ambulanza/della polizia/dei pompieri?
Is there anybody here who speaks English/Italian?
C'è qualcuno che parla inglese/italiano?
I need an interpreter.
Ho bisogno di un interprete.
I have just had an accident.
Ho avuto un incidente.
I have just seen an accident.
Ho assistito a un incidente.
There has been a flood.
Si è verificato un allagamento.
There has been a short circuit/a fire.
Si è verificato un corto circuito/un incendio.
There has been a cave-in/an explosion.
Si è verificato un crollo/uno scoppio.

> Può darmi l'indirizzo/le coordinate?
> Can you give me the address/the whereabouts?

There are severe casualties.
Ci sono feriti gravi.
Don't move him/her/it!
Non muovetelo/la!

145

4.1 EMERGENCIES

He/She isn't breathing.
Non respira.

I have been run over.
Sono stato investito.

My/His/Her blood group is … .
Il mio/suo gruppo sanguigno è … .

Take me to the Emergency Room.
Portatemi al pronto soccorso.

Please call an ambulance/a doctor.
Chiamate un'ambulanza/un medico.

Please call the police/the fire brigade.
Chiamate la polizia/i pompieri.

Would you give me your name and address, please?
Per favore mi dia il suo nome e il suo indirizzo.

■ DANGER SIGNS

Uscita d'emergenza.
Emergency exit.

Bocca antincendio.
Fire hydrant.

In caso di emergenza rompere il vetro.
Break glass in emergency.

Non usare l'ascensore in caso di incendio.
In the event of fire, do not use the lift.

Pericolo. Alta tensione.
Danger. High tension.

VEHICLE BREAKDOWN AND REPAIR

For phrases regarding refuelling, level checks and small repairs that one can handle alone or at a service station, see Area 2.2. The vocabulary here refers to 2-wheel and 4-wheel vehicles.

breakdown lorry	carro attrezzi	'karro at'trettsi
car electrician	elettrauto	elet'trauto
carburettor specialist	carburatorista	karburato'rista
coach builder	carrozziere	karrot'tsjɛre
mechanic	meccanico	mek'kaniko
repair garage	autoofficina	autoffi'tʃina
repair	riparazione	riparat'tsjone
spare part	pezzo di ricambio	'pɛttso diri'kambjo
towing cable/ hitch	cavo/gancio di traino	'kavo/'gantʃo di'traino

■ CAR PARTS

bonnet	cofano	'kɔfano
boot	bagagliaio	bagaʎ'ʎajo
bumper	paraurti	para'urti
chassis	scocca	'skɔkka
door	sportello	spor'tɛllo
fog-guard lamp	fendinebbia	fɛndi'nebbja
fore carriage	avantreno	avan'trɛno
grille	mascherina	maske'rina
handle bar	manubrio	ma'nubrjo
handle	maniglia	ma'niʎʎa
head lamps	fari	'fari
indicator lights/ blinkers	indicatori di direzione	indika'tori didiret'tsjone
knob	manopola	ma'nɔpola
light	luce	lutʃe
side light	di posizione	dipozit'tsjone
reverse light	di retromarcia	dirɛtro'martʃa

147

4.1 EMERGENCIES

lock	serratura	serra'tura
platform	pianale	pja'nale
rear axle	retrotreno	rɛtro'treno
rear view mirror	specchietto retrovisore	spek'kjetto rɛtrovi'zore
rear window	lunotto	lu'nɔtto
registration plate	targa	'targa
roof	tetto	'tetto
seat	sellino	sel'lino
side window	finestrino	fines'trino
stand	cavalletto	kaval'letto
stop light	stop	stɔp
vent window	deflettore	deflet'tore
windscreen	parabrezza	para'breddza
windscreen-wipers	spazzole del tergicristalli	'spattsole deltɛrdʒikris'talli
wing/mudguard	parafango	para'fango

■ MECHANICS AND ELECTRICAL SYSTEM

axle shaft	semiasse	semi'asse
battery	batteria	batte'ria
battery ignition	spinterogeno	spinte'rɔdʒeno
belt	cinghia	'tʃingja
brakes	freni	'frɛni
bushing	bronzina	bron'dzina
cable	cavetto	ka'vetto
camshaft	albero a camme	'albero ak'kamme
carburettor	carburatore	karbura'tore
chain	catena	ka'tena
clutch	frizione	frit'tsjone
connecting rod	biella	'bjɛlla
cooling	raffreddamento	raffredda'mento
water cooling	ad acqua	a'dakkwa
air cooling	ad aria	a'darja
coupling	manicotto	mani'kɔtto

148

English	Italian	Pronunciation
cylinder	cilindro	tʃi'lindro
differential	differenziale	differen'tsjale
distributor points	puntine dello spinterogeno	pun'tine dello spinte'rɔdʒeno
dynamo	alternatore	alterna'tore
electric circuit	circuito elettrico	tʃir'kuito e'lɛttriko
engine	motore	mo'tore
fan	ventola	'vɛntola
fly wheel	volano	vo'lano
gear	marcia	'martʃa
gear-box	cambio	'kambjo
goose-neck	collo d'oca	'kɔllo 'dɔka
head gasket	guarnizione della testata	gwarnit'tsjone dellates'tata
head	testata	tes'tata
hydraulic brake circuit	circuito idraulico dei freni	tʃir'kuito i'drauliko dei'freni
injection	iniezione	injet'tsjone
injector	iniettore	injet'tore
lubrication	lubrificazione	lubrifikat'tsjone
manifold	collettore	kollet'tore
piston	pistone	pis'tone
plug	tappo	'tappo
power	alimentazione	alimentat'tsjone
power brake	servofreno	sɛrvo'freno
power steering	servosterzo	sɛrvos'tɛrtso
radiator	radiatore	radja'tore
reservoir	vaschetta	vas'ketta
cooling liquid reservoir	del liquido refrigerante	del'likwido refridʒe'rante
brake fluid reservoir	dell'olio freni	del'ɔljo 'freni
windscreen washer spray reservoir	del tergicristallo	deltɛrdʒi'kris'tallo

4.1 EMERGENCIES

reverse gear	retromarcia	*retro'martʃa*
rim	cerchione	*tʃer'kjone*
rings	fasce elastiche	*'faʃʃe e'lastike*
shock absorber	ammortizzatore	*ammortiddza'tore*
silencer	marmitta	*mar'mitta*
spark plug	candela	*kan'dela*
spokes	raggi	*'raddʒi*
spring	molla	*'mɔlla*
starter	accensione	*attʃen'sjone*
starting	motorino	*moto'rino*
motor	d'avviamento	*davvia'mento*
steering	sterzo	*'stɛrtso*
suspension	sospensioni	*sospen'sjoni*
tank	serbatoio	*serba'tojo*
thermostat	termostato	*ter'mɔstato*
transmission	albero	*'albero*
shaft	di trasmissione	*ditrazmis'sjone*
tyre	pneumatico	*pneu'matiko*
valve	valvola	*'valvola*
suction valve	di aspirazione	*diaspirat'tsjone*
exhaust valve	di scarico	*dis'kariko*
water pump	pompa dell'acqua	*'pompa del'lakkwa*
fuel pump	del carburante	*delkarbu'rante*
oil pump	dell'olio	*del'lɔljo*
wheel	ruota	*'rwɔta*

■ INTERIORS AND COMMANDS

accelerator	acceleratore	*attʃelera'tore*
brake pedal	pedale del freno	*pe'dale del'freno*
clutch pedal	della frizione	*dellafrit'tsjone*
burglar alarm	antifurto	*anti'furto*
car radio	autoradio	*auto'radjo*
dashboard	cruscotto	*krus'kɔtto*
gear lever	leva del cambio	*'lɛva del'kambjo*
hand brake	freno a mano	*'freno am'mano*

hazard flasher	lampeggiatore	lampeddʒa'tore
ignition key	chiave	'kjave
	di accensione	diattʃen'sjone
odometer	contachilometri	kontaki'lɔmetri
panel	quadro	'kwadro
pedal crank	pedale della	pe'dale
	messa in moto	della'messa in'mɔto
rev counter	contagiri	konta'dʒiri
seatbelt	cintura	tʃin'tura
	di sicurezza	disiku'rettsa
speedometer	tachimetro	ta'kimetro
steering wheel	volante	vo'lante
switch for	interruttore fari	interrut'tore 'fari
side lamps	di posizione	dipozit'tsjone
high-beam	abbaglianti	abbaʎ'ʎanti
head lamps		
dimmer	anabbaglianti	anabbaʎ'ʎanti
head lamps		
warning light	spia	'spia
fuel gauge	livello carburante	li'vɛllo karbu'rante
water temperature	temperatura	tempera'tura
gauge	acqua	'akkwa
oil pressure gauge	pressione olio	pres'sjone 'ɔljo
windscreen washer	lavavetro	lava'vetro

Where can I find a repair garage/a coach builder?
Dove si trova un'autofficina/una carrozeria?
Where can I find a car electrician/a tyre repairer?
Dove si trova un elettrauto/un gommaio?
What is the road assistance number, please?
Qual è il numero del soccorso stradale?
I need a breakdown lorry.
Ho bisogno di un carro-attrezzi.
The car is at Mile/Kilometre … on the … motor way.
La macchina si trova al Km … dell'autostrada … .

4.1 EMERGENCIES

My car won't start.
La mia macchina non parte.
I have run out of fuel.
Sono rimasto senza benzina.
Smoke is coming out of the engine.
Esce fumo dal motore.
The engine is pinking/is back-firing.
Il motore batte in testa/ha dei ritorni di fiamma.
The engine is chugging/proceeds in stops and starts.
Il motore scoppietta/va a singhiozzo.
The engine gets overheated/is making a strange noise.
Il motore surriscalda/fa uno strano rumore.
The brakes are not working.
Non funzionano i freni.
The tank/radiator is leaking.
Il serbatoio/radiatore perde.
The water/oil gauge warning light keeps coming on.
Si accende la spia dell'acqua/dell'olio.
I have a flat tyre.
Ho una gomma a terra.
The boot/bonnet/window/door won't open.
Non si apre il bagagliaio/cofano/finestrino/lo sportello.
The main beam/dimmer head lamps ...
Gli abbaglianti/gli anabbaglianti ...
The stop/indicator lights ...
Gli stop/ le frecce ...
The windscreen wipers/The fog guard lamps ...
I tergicristalli/i fendinebbia ...
... don't work.
... non funzionano.
The clutch is stiff/slips.
La frizione è dura/slitta.

THE MECHANIC'S DIAGNOSIS

Le punterie/la fase/il minimo …
The tappet/stroke/idling speed …

Il gioco della frizione …
The clutch clearance …

La tensione delle cinghie …
The belt tension …

… è da regolare.
… needs adjusting.

Torni fra un quarto d'ora/mezz'ora.
Come back in a quarter of/half an hour.

Il cavo del freno a mano/le ganasce dei freni …
The hand-brake cable/The brake shoe …

L'olio del cambio …
The gear oil …

La scatola dello sterzo …
The steering box …

… è da cambiare.
… needs changing.

Bisogna smontare la frizione/la scatola del cambio.
The clutch/gear case will have to be disassembled.

Debbo sostituire …
I'll have to replace …

… la batteria/le candele/le puntine.
… the battery/the spark plugs/the points.

… le guarnizioni dei freni.
… the braking gaskets.

Devo pulire il carburatore.
The carburettor needs cleaning.

Il disco della frizione/il motorino d'avviamento …
The clutch disc/The starting motor …

La pompa dell'acqua/della benzina …
The water pump/petrol pump …

4.1 EMERGENCIES

Un cuscinetto/un pistone ...
A bearing/A piston ...
... si è bloccato/a .
... has got stuck.

L'alternatore/guarnizione della testata ...
The alternator/head gasket ...
Un fusibile/una valvola ...
A fuse/A valve ...
... si è bruciato/a .
... has burnt out.
Il termostato ...
The thermostat ...
La calotta dello spinterogeno ...
The battery ignition plug ...
La cinghia del ventilatore ...
The fan belt ...
La corda dell'acceleratore/della frizione ...
The accelerator/clutch cable ...
... si è rotto/a .
... has broken.
Il monoblocco ...
The cylinder block ...
La coppa dell'olio/un giunto ...
The oil pump/A coupling ...
... si è spaccato/a.
... has split.
Il piantone dello sterzo/il telaio ...
The steering column/chassis ...
L'albero di trasmissione/la testata ...
The transmission shaft/The head ...
... si è storto/a.
... is bent.
Le fasce elastiche sono usurate.
The rings are worn.

Could you give me an estimate of the cost, please?
Mi può fare un preventivo della spesa?
Do you keep original spare parts?
Avete ricambi originali?

> **Non abbiamo il pezzo di ricambio.**
> We don't have the relevant spare part.

Could you make this repair, please?
Può fare questa riparazione?
Can you tell me who could do it?
Può indicarmi qualcuno che la possa fare?
Could you fix it so that I can at least get to … ?
Può aggiustarla per farmi arrivare fino a … ?

> **No, la sua auto non può marciare.**
> No, I'm afraid your car isn't serviceable.

How long will it take to repair?
Quanto tempo ci vuole per ripararla?
Can I have a detailed invoice, please?
Posso avere una fattura dettagliata?

ROAD ACCIDENTS

To call an ambulance or doctor in the case of an accident with casualties, see Calamity and Dangers (above) and Health. For phrases relative to traffic violations, see also Area 2.2.

collision	tamponamento	tampona'mento
crash	scontro	'skontro
head-on crash	frontale	fron'tale
sideways-on crash	laterale	late'rale
line	linea	'linea
continuous line	continua	kon'tinwa
broken line	tratteggiata	tratted'dʒata

overspeeding	eccesso di velocità	*et'tʃɛsso* *divelot'ʃi'ta*
overtaking	sorpasso	*sor'passo*
priority	precedenza	*pretʃe'dɛntsa*

Are you all right?
Sta/state bene?

We must put out the red warning triangle.
Dobbiamo mettere il triangolo.

I'll go and get the police.
Vado/a a chiamare la polizia.

Hello, the police, please. There has been an accident …
Pronto, polizia. C'è stato un incidente …

 … in … Street/Square, on the corner with … Street.
 … in via/piazza … angolo via … .

 … on the road from … to … at mile number … .
 … sulla strada da … a … al km … .

 … on Motor way number … at mile number … .
 … sull'autostrada n. … al km … .

Non spostate le macchine fino al nostro arrivo.
Do not move the cars until we get there.

Ci sono feriti?
Are there any casualties?

Yes, there is one slight/severe casualty.
Sì, c'è un ferito leggero/grave.

Yes, there are casualties.
Sì, ci sono dei feriti.

No, there is no casualty.
No, nessun ferito.

Did anyone see how the accident happened?
Qualcuno ha veduto come si è svolto l'incidente?

Are you willing to testify?
Lei è disponibile a testimoniare?

May I have your name and address, please?
Posso avere il suo nome e il suo indirizzo?

It's your/his/her fault.
La responsabilità è sua.

I was proceeding in a normal way.
Procedevo regolarmente per la mia strada.

His/Her/Its lights were off.
Aveva i fari spenti.

He/She/It crossed on a red light.
È passato con il rosso.

He came out of the parking lot without looking.
È uscito dal parcheggio senza guardare.

He encroached upon my lane when overtaking.
Sorpassando ha invaso la mia carreggiata.

He turned left/right without giving any warning.
Ha svoltato senza mettere la freccia.

He was not keeping a safe distance.
Non ha rispettato la distanza di sicurezza.

He did not give me priority.
Non mi ha dato la precedenza.

I am sorry. It was my fault.
Sono spiacente, la responsabilità è mia.

I'll write down my particulars and those of my insurance.
Le scrivo i miei dati e i dati dell'assicurazione.

May I see your driving licence/insurance, please?
Posso vedere la sua patente/assicurazione?

What is your registration plate number?
Qual è il suo numero di targa?

You were driving under the effects of alcohol.
Lei stava guidando in stato di ubriachezza.

I was proceeding slowly.
Stavo andando piano.

I have witnesses.
Ho dei testimoni.

MISSING PERSONS

For the loss or theft of documents, tickets, credit cards, travellers cheques, purses, baggage, etc., see Theft Area 4.2 and the Airport Area 2.1.

My name is … .
Il mio nome è … .
I have lost … . Could you make an announcement over the loudspeaker, please?
Ho perduto … , può fare un annuncio con l'altoparlante?
   … my son/my husband/my family …
   … mio figlio/mio marito/la mia famiglia …
   … my group/my guide …
   … il mio gruppo/la mia guida …
My son has got lost. He is a child of … years, dressed in … .
Mio figlio si è perso. È un bambino di … anni, è vestito con … .
Could you call Mr. … over the loudspeaker, please?
Mi può chiamare il Sig. … con l'altoparlante?

THEFT AND MUGGINGS

In case of theft or loss, we advise you to have photocopies of important documents or to keep note of the relative numbers; for theft or loss of purses and baggage, we advise you to prepare a description of the relative contents. Should you have difficulty in communicating, we recommend the assistance of an interpreter.

Help! Stop thief!
Aiuto! Al ladro!
Call the police!
Chiamate la polizia!
Where is the British consulate, please?
Dov'è il consolato britannico?
Where is the lost property office, please?
Dov'è l'ufficio oggetti smarriti?
Where is the police station, please?
Dov'è la stazione di polizia?
I need an interpreter/lawyer.
Ho bisogno di un interprete/avvocato.
I'd like to report the theft/loss ...
Voglio denunciare il furto/lo smarrimento ...
    ... of (my) papers/(my) passport.
    ... dei documenti/del passaporto.
    ... of (my) traveller's cheques/(my) credit card/s.
    ... dei travellers' cheques/della/e carta/e di credito.
    ... of (my) plane ticket.
    ... del biglietto aereo.
    ... of my luggage.
    ... del mio bagaglio.
    ... of (my) wallet/(my) bag.
    ... del portafoglio/della borsa.
I have been mugged.
Sono stato scippato.

4.2 THEFT, DAMAGE, ASSAULT

Aveva denaro/preziosi/oggetti di valore?
Did you have any money/jewels/valuables on you?
Ci sono testimoni?
Are there any witnesses?
In quanti erano?
How many of them were there?
Dove aveva l'oggetto?
Where was the object when it was stolen/lost?

I had it in my bag/in the car.
Lo avevo in borsa/in macchina.
I had it in my hand/in my pocket.
Lo avevo in mano/in tasca.

Mi descriva l'oggetto rubato/smarrito.
Please describe the stolen/lost object.
Saprebbe descrivere/riconoscere il ladro?
Would you be able to describe/recognize the thief?

My car has been stolen. It was parked in … .
Mi hanno rubato la macchina, era parcheggiata in … .
The car window was broken and my … stolen.
Hanno rotto il finestrino dell'auto e mi hanno rubato … .

Dov'è avvenuto il furto?
Where did the theft take place?

The theft took place in … .
Il furto è avvenuto in … .

Vuole sporgere denuncia?
Do you want to make a statement?

THEFT, DAMAGE, ASSAULT 4.2

DAMAGES

Useful phrases should you suffer or provoke damage to things (stain a garment, break an object, etc.).

compensation	indennizzo	*inden'niddzo*
damage	danno	*'danno*
insurance	assicurazione	*assikurat'tsjone*
loss	perdita	*'pɛrdita*
refund	risarcimento	*risartʃi'mento*
repair	riparazione	*riparat'tsjone*

You have broken my … .
Lei mi ha rotto … .
You have stained my … .
Lei mi ha macchiato … .
I must insist on your compensating me.
Lei mi deve risarcire.
Please give me your name and address.
Mi lasci il suo nome e indirizzo.
I will forward the invoice to your home address.
Le manderò la fattura a casa.
Are you insured?
Lei è assicurato?
I did not do it on purpose.
Non l'ho fatto apposta.
I did not see you.
Non l'avevo vista.
Where can I get … repaired?
Dove posso far riparare. … ?

4.2 THEFT, DAMAGE, ASSAULT

If you happen to hit or damage a parked car in the absence of its owner, you should leave a signed note to this effect:

I have bumped into your car. Please call me at number … .
Ho urtato la sua auto, mi chiami al numero … .

AGGRESSIONS AND ASSAULTS

Should you have difficulty in communicating, we recommend the assistance of an interpreter.

Leave me alone!
Mi lasci in pace!
Go away, or I'll call the police!
Se ne vada o chiamo la polizia!
Stop following me, or I'll call the police!
Smetta di seguirmi o chiamo la polizia!
Help! There's a man following me!
Aiuto, c'è un uomo che mi sta seguendo!
Help! There's a man bothering me!
Aiuto, c'è un uomo che mi molesta!
I'd like to report a case of assault.
Vorrei denunciare un'aggressione.
I'd like to report a case of attempted rape.
Vorrei denunciare un tentativo di violenza.

> **Dove è accaduto?**
> Where did it happen?
> **Quanti erano?**
> How many of them were there?
> **Saprebbe riconoscerlo/i?**
> Would you be able to recognize him/them?
> **C'erano testimoni?**
> Were there any witnesses?

FINDING YOUR BEARINGS IN THE CITY

These words and phrases will help you ask for directions in the city or town you are visiting, be you on foot or in a car. To request directions for longer distances, see Area 2.2 (Car).

bend	curva	'kurva
block	isolato	izo'lato
crossing	attraversamento	attraversa'mento
crossroads	incrocio	in'krotʃo
fly over	cavalcavia	kavalka'via
illuminated sign	insegna luminosa	in'seɲɲa lumi'nosa
pedestrian crossing	passaggio pedonale	pas'saddʒo pedo'nale
roundabout	rotatoria	rota'tɔrja
street number	numero civico	'numero 'tʃiviko
subway	sottopassaggio	sottopas'saddʒo
traffic lights	semaforo	se'maforo
tunnel	tunnel	'tunnel

Can you tell me where ... Street is, please?
Dov'è via ... ?

> **Sempre a diritto.**
> Straight on.
> **Giri a destra/sinistra al ... incrocio/semaforo.**
> Turn right/left at the ... crossroads/traffic lights.
> **È a ... isolati da qui.**
> It is ... blocks away from here.
> **Continui a diritto fino all'inizio di ... , e lì domandi di nuovo.**
> Keep straight on till you get to ... and ask again.
> **È in fondo alla strada.**
> It is at the bottom of the road.
> **Ha una cartina?**
> Have you got a street plan?

4.3 BEARINGS

Can you show me where ... Road is on the map, please?
Mi può indicare sulla cartina dov'è via ... ?
I have to go to ... Street. Could you make a sketch of the route, please?
Debbo andare in via ... . Può farmi uno schizzo del percorso?
Could you write down the address, please?
Mi può scrivere l'indirizzo?
Which district of the city/town are we in?
In che zona della città siamo?
Can you tell me how to get back into the centre, please?
Come faccio a tornare in centro?

> **Deve tornare indietro.**
> You'll have to turn back.

What is the shortest way to ... , please?
Qual è la strada più breve per andare a ... ?
Can one walk to ... ?
È possibile andare a piedi a ... ?

> **È molto lontano, non può andare a piedi.**
> It is a very long way. You can't go on foot.

Can one get to ... by car/bus?
È possibile andare in macchina/autobus a ... ?

> **È zona pedonale, non può arrivarci in macchina.**
> It is a pedestrian precinct. Cars are not permitted.

Can you tell me how far away ... Street is?
Quanto dista via ... ?
Am I going in the right direction for ... ?
È questa la direzione giusta per ... ?
Can you tell me where I can buy a plan of the town(city)/public transport?
Dove posso comprare una cartina della città/dei mezzi di trasporto?

Warning: if you are allergic to any drug or treatment, it is a good idea to learn its name in Italian before ever having to put it to use, so that you may inform quickly the doctor who is treating you, rather than wasting precious time searching for its translation in an emergency situation.

ILLNESS AND SYMPTOMS

ache	male	'male
tooth ache	di denti	di'dɛnti
sore throat	di gola	di'gola
ear ache	d'orecchi	do'rekki
tummy ache	di pancia	di'pantʃa
stomach ache	di stomaco	dis'tɔmako
headache	di testa	di'tɛsta
anaemia	anemia	ane'mia
appendicitis	appendicite	appendi'tʃite
arthritis	artrite	ar'trite
asthma	asma	'azma
bronchitis	bronchite	bron'kite
car sickness	mal d'auto	mal 'dauto
cardiopathy	cardiopatia	kardjopa'tia
catarrh	catarro	ka'tarro
cerebral haemorrhage	emorragia cerebrale	emorra'dʒia tʃere'brale
colitis	colite	ko'lite
collapse	collasso	kol'lasso
coma	coma	'kɔma
congestion	congestione	kondʒes'tjone
conjunctivitis	congiuntivite	kondʒunti'vite
constipation	stitichezza	stiti'kettsa
cough	tosse	'tosse
cramp	crampo	'krampo
cystitis	cistite	tʃis'tite
diabetes	diabete	dja'bɛte
diphtheria	difterite	difte'rite

dysentery	dissenteria	dissente'ria
fainting	svenimento	zveni'mento
fever/temperature	febbre	'fɛbbre
frost-bite	congelamento	kondʒela'mento
gastritis	gastrite	gas'trite
gout	gotta	'gotta
haematoma	ematoma	ema'tɔma
haemorrhage	emorragia	emorra'dʒia
heart attack	infarto	in'farto
heartburn	acidità	atʃidi'ta
	di stomaco	dis'tɔmako
hepatic colic	colica di fegato	'kɔlika di'fegato
hepatitis	epatite	epa'tite
herpes	erpes	'ɛrpes
high blood	pressione alta	pres'sjone 'alta
pressure		
low b.p.	bassa	'bassa
ictus	ictus	'iktus
infection	infezione	infet'tsjone
intoxication	intossicazione	intossikat'tsjone
jaundice	itterizia	itte'rittsja
kidney colic	colica di reni	'kɔlika di'rɛni
laryngitis	laringite	larin'dʒite
leukemia	leucemia	leutʃe'mia
lumbago	lombaggine	lom'baddʒine
malaise	malessere	ma'lɛssere
malaria	malaria	ma'larja
migraine	emicrania	emi'kranja
mountain sickness	mal di montagna	mal dimon'taɲɲa
nephritis	nefrite	ne'frite
neuralgia	nevralgia	nevral'dʒia
otitis	otite	o'tite
palpitations	palpitazioni	palpitat'tsjoni
paralysis	paralisi	pa'ralizi
period pains	dolori mestruali	do'lori mestru'ali

peritonitis	peritonite	perito'nite
pleurisy	pleurite	pleu'rite
pneumonia	polmonite	polmo'nite
rheumatism	reumatismo	reuma'tizmo
sciatica	sciatica	'ʃatika
smarting	bruciore	bru'tʃore
sneezing	starnuto	star'nuto
suffocation	soffocamento	soffoka'mento
taenia	tenia	'tɛnja
tetanus	tetano	'tɛtano
thrombosis	trombosi	trom'bɔzi
tonsillitis	tonsillite	tonsil'lite
tumour	tumore	tu'more
ulcer	ulcera	'ultʃera
vertigo	vertigini	ver'tidʒini

CONTAGIOUS DISEASES AND VIRAL INFECTIONS

AIDS	AIDS	'aidz
chickenpox	varicella	vari'tʃella
cholera	colera	ko'lɛra
diphtheria	difterite	difte'rite
German measles	rosolia	rozo'lia
measles	morbillo	mor'billo
meningitis	meningite	menin'dʒite
mumps	orecchioni	orek'kjoni
parotitis	parotite	paro'tite
scarlet fever	scarlattina	skarlat'tina
smallpox	vaiolo	va'jɔlo
tuberculosis	tubercolosi	tuberko'lɔzi
typhus	tifo	'tifo
venereal diseases	malattie veneree	malat'tie ve'nɛree
viral hepatitis	epatite virale	epa'tite vi'rale

4.4 HEALTH

TRAUMA

abrasion	abrasione	*abra'zjone*
bite	morsicatura	*morsika'tura*
bruise	contusione	*kontu'zjone*
burn	ustione	*us'tjone*
concussion	commozione	*kommot'tsjone*
of the brain	cerebrale	*tʃere'brale*
cut	taglio	*'taʎʎo*
dislocation	lussazione	*lussat'tsjone*
effusion	versamento	*versa'mento*
electric burn	folgorazione	*folgorat'tsjone*
excoriation	escoriazione	*eskorjat'tsjone*
fracture	frattura	*frat'tura*
haematoma	ematoma	*ema'tɔma*
injury	ferita	*fe'rita*
insect sting	puntura d'insetto	*pun'tura din'sɛtto*
lesion	lesione	*le'zjone*
shock	shock	*ʃɔk*
sprain	distorsione	*distor'sjone*
sunstroke	insolazione	*insolat'tsjone*

PARTS OF THE BODY

ankle	caviglia	*ka'viʎʎa*
appendix	appendice	*appen'ditʃe*
arm	braccio	*'brattʃo*
armpit	ascella	*aʃ'ʃɛlla*
artery	arteria	*ar'tɛrja*
articulation	articolazione	*artikolat'tsjone*
back	schiena	*'skjɛna*
belly/tummy	pancia	*'pantʃa*
bladder	vescica	*veʃ'ʃika*
blood	sangue	*'sangwe*
bone	osso	*'ɔsso*

breast	seno	'seno
bronchi	bronchi	'bronki
chest	petto	'pɛtto
chin	mento	'mento
collar bone	clavicola	kla'vikola
ear	orecchio	o'rekkjo
elbow	gomito	'gomito
femur	femore	'fɛmore
finger	dito	'dito
foot	piede	'pjɛde
genital organs	organi genitali	'ɔrgani dʒeni'tali
gland	ghiandola	'gjandola
hand	mano	'mano
head	testa	'tɛsta
heart	cuore	'kwɔre
intestine	intestino	intes'tino
jaw	mascella	maʃ'ʃɛlla
kidney	rene	'rɛne
knee	ginocchio	dʒi'nɔkkjo
larynx	laringe	la'rindʒe
leg	gamba	'gamba
lip	labbro	'labbro
liver	fegato	'fegato
lung	polmone	pol'mone
mouth	bocca	'bokka
muscle	muscolo	'muskolo
neck	collo	'kɔllo
nerve	nervo	'nɛrvo
nose	naso	'naso
nostril	narice	na'ritʃe
oesophagus	esofago	e'zɔfago
ovary	ovaia	o'vaja
palate	palato	pa'lato
pelvis	bacino	ba'tʃino
penis	pene	'pɛne

4.4 HEALTH

fibula	perone	pe'rone
pharynx	faringe	fa'rindʒe
pulse	polso	'polso
rib	costola	'kɔstola
shoulder	spalla	'spalla
side/hip	fianco	'fjanko
skin	pelle	'pɛlle
skull	cranio	'kranjo
spleen	milza	'miltsa
stomach	stomaco	'stɔmako
tendon	tendine	'tɛndine
thigh	coscia	'kɔʃʃa
throat	gola	gola
tibia	tibia	'tibja
toe	dito	'dito
tongue	lingua	'lingwa
tonsil	tonsilla	ton'silla
vagina	vagina	va'dʒina
vein	vena	'vena
vertebra	vertebra	'vɛrtebra
vertebral column	colonna vertebrale	ko'lonna verte'brale
womb	utero	'utero

ASKING FOR MEDICAL ASSISTANCE

I feel ill.
Mi sento male.
I need a doctor.
Ho bisogno di un medico.
I'd like to call a paediatrician.
Vorrei chiamare un pediatra.
Is there a doctor in the hotel/camping site?
C'è un medico in albergo/nel campeggio?
Would it be possible to have an English-speaking doctor?
Si può trovare un medico che parli inglese?
Can the doctor come visiting here?
Il medico può venire a visitare qui?
Please call an ambulance.
Chiamate un'ambulanza.
Where is the surgery?
Dov'è l'ambulatorio?
Where is there a hospital?
Dov'è un ospedale?
Where is there a first-aid station?
Dov'è un pronto soccorso?

4.4 HEALTH

SPEAKING WITH A DOCTOR

*The phrases can refer to oneself or to others who are unable to speak;
a child, for example.*

I have/He/She has had a temperature for ... hours.
Ho/ha ... di febbre da ... ore.
**I have/He/She has eaten/drunk something which has made
me/him/her ill.**
Ho/ha mangiato/bevuto qualcosa che mi/gli/le ha fatto male.

> **Che cosa ha mangiato/bevuto?**
> What have you eaten/drunk?
> **Si stenda qui.**
> Lie down here.
> **Si spogli.**
> Get undressed.
> **Che cosa si sente?**
> What do you feel?

I have a general sense of malaise.
Avverto un malessere generale.
My head is spinning.
Mi gira la testa.
I feel weak.
Mi sento debole.
I have/He/She has ...
Ho/ha ...

> **... got the shivers/the cramps.**
> ... i brividi/ i crampi.
> **... got a cold/the flu.**
> ... il raffreddore/l'influenza.
> **... got indigestion/diarrhea/nausea.**
> ... l'indigestione/la diarrea/la nausea.
> **... got haemorrhoids/a nasty itch.**
> ... le emorroidi/un forte prurito.

... got a hernia/an abscess.
... un'ernia/un ascesso.
... vomited.
... vomitato.
I have developed ...
Mi è venuto/a ...
... a spot/a swelling.
... uno sfogo/un gonfiore.
... a rash/eczema.
... un'eruzione/un eczema.
... an irritation/an inflammation.
... un'irritazione/un'infiammazione.

Dove sente male?
Where does it hurt?

All over.
Dappertutto.
My joints/arms/legs ...
Le articolazioni/le braccia/le gambe ...
My head/eyes ...
La testa/gli occhi...
My teeth ...
I denti ...
My tummy/stomach ...
La pancia/lo stomaco...
... ache/aches.
... mi fa/fanno male.
My ears are/throat is sore.
Le orecchie/la gola mi fanno/fa male.
My back/chest hurts.
Mi fa male la schiena/il petto.

Che genere di dolore è?
What kind of pain is it?

4.4 HEALTH

It is … pain.
È un dolore …

>   **… a sharp/a dull/a throbbing …**
>   … acuto/sordo/molto forte.
>   **… an intermittent/a persistent …**
>   … intermittente/persistente.

Da quanto tempo avverte il dolore?
How long has it/have they been hurting?
Le fa male qui?
Does it hurt here?
Ha già preso delle medicine?
Have you already taken any medicine?
Apra la bocca.
Open your mouth.
La devo auscultare.
I'll have to examine you with the stethoscope.
Respiri profondamente.
Take a deep breath.
Tossisca.
Cough.
Si giri.
Turn over/round.
Le misurerò la pressione.
I'll take your blood pressure.

Is it contagious?
È contagioso?
Is it serious?
È grave?
Would you point to the name of the illness on this list, please?
Può indicarmi il nome della malattia su questa lista?

>   **Non si preoccupi, non è niente di grave.**
>   Don't worry. It's nothing serious.

I suffer/He/She suffers from … .
Soffro/e di … .
I am/He/She is allergic to … .
Sono/È allergico a … .
I am/He/She is a diabetic.
Sono/È diabetico.

> **Qual è la sua dose normale di insulina?**
> What is the dose of insulin you/he/she usually take/s?
> **Per via orale o endovenosa?**
> Orally or by intravenous injection?

I am … months pregnant.
Sono incinta di … mesi.

> **Prenda questo … volte al giorno per … giorni prima/durante/dopo i pasti.**
> Take this … times a day for … days before/during/after meals.
> **Le prescriverò un antibiotico.**
> I'll prescribe an antibiotic for you.
> **Le faccio una ricetta per andare in farmacia.**
> I'll write a prescription for the chemist.
> **Rimanga a letto fino a quando non sarà passata la febbre.**
> Stay in bed until the fever has gone down.
> **Lei ha bisogno di uno specialista.**
> You need a specialist doctor.
> **Stia a digiuno per … giorni.**
> Fast for … days.
> **Mangi leggero/in bianco.**
> Keep your diet light/Keep off heavily-seasoned foods.
> **Deve fare un enteroclisma.**
> You'll have to have an enema.
> **Non esca.**
> Do not go outside.
> **Deve sottoporsi a un prelievo del sangue/dell'urina/delle feci.**
> You'll have to do a test on your blood/urine/faeces.

4.4 HEALTH

Devo farle un'iniezione ...
I must give you an ... (1) injection ... (2) .
... di antibiotico/antitetanica.
... (1) antibiotic/anti tetanus ...
... calmante contro il dolore.
... (2) to ease the pain.
Devo ricoverarla in ospedale.
You'll have to stay in hospital for a little.

Could you inform my family, please?
Potrebbe avvertire la mia famiglia?
Can I continue on my journey?
Posso continuare il viaggio?

■ MEDICAL SPECIALISTS

dentist	dentista	*den'tista*
ear, nose and throat specialist	otorino- laringoiatra	*otorino- laringo'jatra*
gynaecologist	ginecologo	*dʒine'kɔlogo*
optician	oculista	*oku'lista*
orthopaedist	ortopedico	*orto'pɛdiko*
paediatrician	pediatra	*pe'djatra*
psychiatrist	psichiatra	*psi'kjatra*
psychologist	psicologo	*psi'kɔlogo*
veterinary surgeon	veterinario	*veteri'narjo*

ANXIETY AND SIMILAR STATES

I feel very agitated.
Mi sento molto agitato.
I suffer from bouts of anxiety.
Ho crisi di ansia.
I can't sleep.
Non riesco a dormire.
I suffer from insomnia and a poor appetite.
Ho insonnia e disappetenza.
I feel depressed.
Mi sento depresso.
Can you prescribe ... for me, please?
Può prescrivermi ...

> **... a sleeping pill/a sedative ...**
> ... un sonnifero/un sedativo?
> **... an anxiolytic/a tranquillizer ...**
> ... un ansiolitico/un tranquillante?

> **Ha già preso medicinali?**
> Have you already taken any medicament?
> **Lei è in cura per questi sintomi?**
> Are you already being treated for these symptoms?
> **Usa già un medicinale abituale?**
> Do you already have any drugs which you usually take?

Could you write me out a prescription for this medicine?
Può farmi una ricetta per questo medicinale?

> **Questo non esiste da noi, le prescrivo un equivalente.**
> That one is not available here. I'll prescribe an equivalent
> medicine.

4.4 HEALTH

THE DENTIST, THE ORTHODONTIST

canine tooth	canino	*ka'nino*
decay	carie	*'karje*
extraction	estrazione	*estrat'tsjone*
gum	gengiva	*dʒen'dʒiva*
incisor	incisivo	*intʃi'zivo*
molar	molare	*mo'lare*
premolar	premolare	*premo'lare*
wisdom tooth	dente del giudizio	*'dɛnte deldʒu'ditts*

Could you recommend a dentist?
Mi può consigliare un dentista?
I'd like to make an appointment with Doctor ... , please.
Vorrei prendere un appuntamento con il dottor ... .

> **Per quando?**
> When for?

As soon as possible, please. It's urgent.
Prima possibile. È urgente.
I have terrible toothache.
Ho un forte mal di denti.
This tooth hurts.
Mi fa male questo dente.
I've got an abscess.
Ho un ascesso.
One of my fillings has come out.
Mi si è rotta un'otturazione.
I have broken a tooth.
Mi si è rotto un dente.
Can you give me something for the pain?
Mi può dare qualcosa contro il dolore?

> **Tenga la bocca ben aperta.**
> Keep your mouth wide open.

Il dente è cariato.
The tooth is decayed.
Lei ha un ascesso.
You have got an abscess.
Il suo dente va ...
Your tooth must be ...
... otturato/ricostruito.
... filled/rebuilt.
... tolto/devitalizzato.
... taken out/devitalized.

Can you deal with it temporarily?
Può fare un lavoro provvisorio?

Le devo estrarre il dente.
I must extract the tooth.
Le devo trapanare il dente.
I must drill the tooth.
Le faccio un'anestesia locale.
I'll give you a local anaesthetic.
Le farò male per pochi secondi.
It will hurt for a few seconds.

I have broken my ...
Mi si è rotta/o ...
... dental plate.
... l'apparecchio.
... crown.
... la capsula.
... denture.
... la dentiera.
Can you repair it?
Può ripararla/o?
Can you repair it for the time being?
Può fare una riparazione provvisoria?

4.4 HEALTH

When will it be ready?
Quando sarà pronta?
Can you give me an estimate of the cost, please?
Mi può fare un preventivo di spesa?

> **Non mastichi da questa parte per qualche ora.**
> Don't chew on that side for a few hours.

THE OPTOMETRIST

I'd like to have my eyes tested.
Vorrei misurarmi la vista.
All of a sudden my eyesight has got worse.
Mi si è improvvisamente abbassata la vista.
I can no longer see properly out of one eye.
Non ci vedo più bene da un occhio.
My vision is blurred/out of focus.
Vedo appannato/sfuocato.
I am astigmatic/short-sighted/far-sighted.
Sono astigmatico/miope/presbite.
My lenses are broken/I've lost my contact lenses.
Ho rotto le lenti/ho perduto le lenti a contatto.
Can you replace them for me, please?
Può sostituirmele?
When will they be ready?
Quando saranno pronte?

MEDICAL BILLS AND PAYMENT

How much do I owe you?
Quanto devo?
Shall I pay you or the nurse?
Pago a lei o all'infermiera?
Could you give me a receipt, please?
Può rilasciarmi ricevuta?

THE EMERGENCY ROOM

■ **PHRASES USEFUL DURING THE AMBULANCE RIDE
AND IN THE EMERGENCY ROOM OF A HOSPITAL.**

I fell.
Sono caduto.
I banged my ...
Ho battuto ...

> **... hip/coccyx.**
> ... il bacino/il coccige.
> **... thigh-bone/kneecap.**
> ... il femore/il ginocchio.
> **... elbow/back.**
> ... il gomito/la schiena.
> **... head.**
> ... la testa.

I had an electric shock.
Ho preso la scossa elettrica.
I've ... myself.
Mi sono ...

> **... pricked/burnt ...**
> ... punto/ustionato.
> **... grazed/cut ...**
> ... scorticato/tagliato.
> **An animal ...**
> Un animale...
> **A dog ...**
> Un cane ...
> **A viper/snake ...**
> Una vipera/un serpente ...

... has bitten me.
... mi ha morso.
An insect has stung me.
Mi ha punto un insetto.

4.4 HEALTH

Could you examine this ...
Può esaminare questo/a ...

> **... lump/swelling?**
> ... bernoccolo/tumefazione?
> **... graze/scratch?**
> ... escoriazione/graffio?
> **... sting/cut?**
> ... puntura/taglio?

I have been in the sun too long.
Ho preso troppo sole.

I have difficulty in breathing.
Faccio fatica a respirare.

I've got something in my eye.
Mi è entrato qualcosa nell'occhio.

I've lost a lot of blood.
Ho perso molto sangue.

My blood group is ... positive/negative.
Il mio gruppo sanguigno è ... positivo/negativo.

> **Le fa male qui?**
> Does it hurt here?
> **Le fa male se premo/tiro/spingo/muovo?**
> Does it hurt if I press/pull/push here/move it?
> **Ha urto di vomito?**
> Do you want to vomit?
> **Alzi il braccio/la gamba finché può.**
> Raise your arm/leg as far as you can.
> **Lei ha ...**
> You have ...
> **... la commozione cerebrale/un trauma cranico.**
> ... a concussion/a head injury.
> **... una contusione/una lussazione.**
> ... a bruise/a dislocation.
> **... una frattura/una slogatura.**
> ... a fracture/a sprain.

... uno strappo muscolare.
... pulled a muscle.

Dobbiamo farle/darle ...
We must give you ...
... un impacco.
... a compress.
... un piccolo intervento.
... a minor operation.
... un'ingessatura.
... a plaster cast.
... una fasciatura stretta/steccata.
... a tight/splinted bandaging.
... una radiografia.
... an X-ray.
... un'anestesia locale/totale.
... a local/general anaesthetic.
... un calmante per il dolore.
... a pain killer.
... dei punti di sutura.
... a few stitches.

Torni fra ... giorni per ...
Come back in ... days ...
... rifare la fasciatura.
... to have a fresh dressing.
... togliere il gesso.
... to have the plaster removed.
... un controllo.
... for a check up.
... togliere i punti.
... to have the stitches taken out.

Dovrà rimanere a letto per qualche giorno.
You'll have to stay in bed for a few days.

4.4 HEALTH

Dobbiamo ricoverarla/o.
You'll have to spend a little time in hospital.

Phrases useful when you are assisting someone who cannot speak for themselves.

He/She has fainted.
È svenuto.
He/She has fallen.
È caduto.
He/She has been run over.
È stato investito.
He/She has had an electric shock.
È stato folgorato.
He/She has had a heart attack.
Ha già avuto un attacco cardiaco.
He/She is prone to ...
È soggetto a ...
    ... convulsions.
    ... convulsioni.
    ... epileptic fits.
    ... crisi epilettiche.
    ... haemorrhages.
    ... emorragie.
He/She is allergic to ...
È allergico a ... .

Abbiamo bisogno dell'autorizzazione di un familiare.
We need the authorization of a member of the family.
La prognosi è riservata.
The prognosis is uncertain.

AT THE CHEMIST'S

analgesic	analgesico	*anal'dʒɛziko*
antibiotic	antibiotico	*antibi'ɔtiko*
antipyretic	antipiretico	*antipi'rɛtiko*
antiseptic	antisettico	*anti'sɛttiko*
aspirin	aspirina	*aspi'rina*
astringent	astringente	*astrin'dʒɛnte*
baby	pomata	*po'mata*
ointment	per neonati	*perneo'nati*
bandage	benda	*'bɛnda*
boiler	bollitore	*bolli'tore*
chemist's	farmacia	*farma'tʃia*
cicatrizant	cicatrizzante	*tʃikatrid'dzante*
condoms	preservativi	*preserva'tivi*
contraceptives	anticoncezionali	*antikontʃettsjo'nali*
cortisone	cortisone	*korti'zone*
digestive	digestivo	*didʒes'tivo*
disinfectant	disinfettante	*dizinfet'tante*
drops	gocce	*'gottʃe*
drug for	farmaco	*'farmako*
intravenous	per via	*per'via*
injections	endovenosa	*endove'nosa*
intramuscular	per via	*per'via*
injections	intramuscolare	*intramusko'lare*
oral use	per via orale	*per'via o'rale*
rectal use	per via rettale	*per'via ret'tale*
elastic	fascia	*'faʃʃa*
bandage	elastica	*e'lastika*
enema	clistere	*klis'tɛre*
eye-wash/	collirio	*kol'lirjo*
drops		
gargle	gargarismo	*garga'rizmo*
headache	cachet	*kaʃʃe*
powder		

hot water bottle	borsa dell'acqua calda	'borsa del'lakkwa 'kalda
injection	iniezione	injet'tsjone
insecticide	insetticida	insetti'tʃida
insulin	insulina	insu'lina
internal tampons	assorbenti igienici interni	assor'bɛnti i'dʒenitʃi in'tɛrni
laxative	lassativo	lassa'tivo
methylated spirits	alcol	'alkol
mouthwash	collutorio	kollu'tɔrjo
ointment	crema	'krɛma
for insect bites	contro le punture	'kontro lepun'ture
for sun-burn	contro le scottature	'kontro leskotta'ture
panty liners	salvaslip	salvaz'lip
plasters	cerotti	tʃe'rɔtti
products	prodotti	pro'dotti
for diabetics	per diabetici	perdja'bɛtitʃi
homeopathic products	omeopatici	omeo'patitʃi
saccharine	saccarina	sakka'rina
sanitary towels/ S.T.'s	assorbenti igienici esterni	assor'bɛnti i'dʒenitʃi es'tɛrni
sedative	calmante/ sedativo	kal'mante/ seda'tivo
sleeping pill	sonnifero	son'nifero
sterile gauze	garza sterile	'gardza 'stɛrile
sterilizing tablets	pasticche sterilizzanti	pas'tikke sterilid'dzanti
suppositories	supposte	sup'poste
syringe	siringa	si'ringa
syrup	sciroppo	ʃi'rɔppo
thermometer	termometro	ter'mɔmetro

tincture of iodine	tintura di iodio	tin'tura di'jɔdjo
tourniquet (haemostat)	laccio emostatico	'lattʃo emos'tatiko
tranquillizer	tranquillante	trankwil'lante
vaccine	vaccino	vat'tʃino
Vaseline	vaselina	vaze'lina
vitamins	vitamine	vita'mine
water	acqua	'akkwa
distilled	distillata	distil'lata
low in mineral content	oligominerale	oligomine'rale
hydrogen peroxide	ossigenata	ossidʒe'nata

Where can I find a chemist's open?
Dov'è una farmacia aperta?

What time do chemists open/close?
A che ora aprono/chiudono le farmacie?

Where is there a chemist's open round the clock/at night/on holidays?
Dov'è una farmacia aperta 24 ore/la notte/i festivi?

I'd like something for …
Vorrei qualcosa contro …

   … tooth ache/a sore throat/a headache.
   … il mal di denti/di gola/di testa.

   … hay fever.
   … il raffreddore da fieno.

   … a cold/flu.
   … il raffreddore/l'influenza.

Are there any contraindications?
Ci sono controindicazioni?

4.4 HEALTH

Is it all right for … sufferers?
Va bene per chi soffre di … ?
I'd like some (name of the drug).
Vorrei del … .
A small pack will do.
Basta una confezione piccola.

> **Non posso darle questo prodotto senza ricetta.**
> This drug can only be handed over if you have a prescription.

Could you make up this preparation, please?
Può fare questa preparazione?
Will I have to wait long?
C'è molto da aspettare?

AREA 5. DISCOVERING

This sections deals with the most typical situations of travelling: that is, visiting the sights and museums, going on excursions, seeing shows and sporting events, outdoor play and pastimes, shopping for necessities and extras. These situations are presented in the utmost detail, both in vocabulary and in phrases, in order to give the traveller the greatest assistance in organising the most exciting and gratifying moments of his trip, particularly in situation 5.4. The vocabulary of this section was compiled with great care, with the intent of providing the widest range possible of articles, so that the most particular traveller might feel at ease while shopping, find exactly what they desire and be in a position to conclude the purchase to their satisfaction.

5.1
MEETING PEOPLE

5.2
SIGHTSEEING
AND TOURS

5.3
ENTERTAINMENT
AND LEISURE

5.4
SHOPPING

5.1 MEETING PEOPLE

THE FIRST APPROACH

Da dove viene?
Where do you come from?

I am English.
Sono inglese.
I'm here ...
Sono qui ...
   ... on holiday/on business.
   ... in vacanza/per lavoro.
   ... to study/for a conference.
   ... per motivi di studio/per un convegno.
I only speak English.
Parlo solo inglese.
I understand just a little Italian.
Capisco solo un po' d'italiano.
I don't understand. Could you repeat that, please?
Non ho capito. Può ripetere?

È la prima volta che viene in ... ?
Is this your first time in ... ?

I have been here once before.
Ci sono già stato un'altra volta.

Dove alloggia?
Where are you staying?

I'm ...
Sono ...
   ... at a hotel/camping site.
   ... in un albergo/campeggio.
   ... staying with a family/friends.
   ... presso una famiglia/in casa d'amici.

Le piace ... ?
Do you like ... ?

Yes, I do./No, I don't.
Sì, mi piace./No, non mi piace.
Is it always so cold/hot?
È sempre così freddo/caldo?
A lovely day today.
Bella giornata oggi.

These are a few useful phrases to approach a "native" speaker. Particular details and the content of the dialogue obviously depend upon the circumstances or specific needs of each case.

Do you speak English?
Parla inglese?
Could you help me, please?
Potrebbe aiutarmi?
Could you speak more slowly/loudly, please?
Può parlare più lentamente/a voce più alta?
Would you write it down, please?
Può scriverlo?
Could you translate what's written, please?
Può tradurmi cosa c'è scritto?

Could you show me the word in the phrase book, please?
Può indicarmi la parola sul frasario?

How do you pronounce it?
Come si pronuncia?

5.1 MEETING PEOPLE

GREETINGS AND INTRODUCTIONS

My name is … .
Mi chiamo … .
May I introduce you to … ?
Posso presentarle … ?
Pleased to meet you.
Piacere di conoscerla.
How are you?
Come sta?
I'm fine, thanks. And you?
Sto bene, grazie e Lei?
All right, thanks.
Non c'è male.
I hope to see you again.
Spero di incontrarla di nuovo.

ACQUAINTANCES AND INVITATIONS

May I come in/join you?
Disturbo?
I have just arrived.
Sono arrivato da poco.
Are you from here?
Lei è del posto?
Where do you live?
Dove abita?
Which country are you from?
Da quale paese viene?
Whereabouts?
Da quale città?
Where are you heading for?
Dove è diretto/a?
Are you staying long?
Si fermerà molto?

Are you also a traveller?
È in viaggio anche lei?

Are you alone?
È sola/o?

Would you like to dance?
Vuole ballare?

Can I offer you something to drink?
Posso invitarla a bere qualcosa?

Would you like to come with me/us …
Verrebbe con me/noi …

… to the theatre/cinema/to a discotheque?
… al teatro/cinema/in discoteca?

… for a walk?
… a fare una passeggiata?

I would like to invite you to dinner.
Vorrei invitarla a cena.

Where can we meet?
Dove possiamo incontrarci?

What's your telephone number?
Qual è il suo numero telefonico?

My telephone number is … .
Il mio numero telefonico è … .

I'll see you at … . I'll fetch you at home/the hotel.
Ci vediamo alle ore …, la verrò a prendere a casa/in albergo.

I hope to see you again.
Spero di incontrarla nuovamente.

It has been a lovely evening.
È stata una splendida serata.

Grazie, preferisco di no.
No, thank you. I'd rather not.

Con piacere.
With pleasure.

Sono impegnato/a.
I'm engaged.

SEEING THE SIGHTS

ancient town	città vecchia	tʃit'ta 'vɛkkja
antiques	antichità	antiki'ta
aquarium	acquario	ak'kwarjo
archaeological site	area archeologica	'area arkeo'lɔdʒika
art gallery	galleria d'arte	galle'ria 'darte
botanic gardens	giardino botanico	dʒar'dino bo'tanike
building	palazzo	pa'lattso
castle	castello	kas'tɛllo
catacombs	catacombe	kata'kombe
cave	grotta	'grɔtta
collection	collezione	kollet'tsjone
commercial centre	centro commerciale	'tʃentro kommer'tʃale
court house	tribunale	tribu'nale
display	mostra	'mostra
excavations	scavi	'skavi
exhibition	esposizione	espozit'tsjone
fair	fiera	'fjɛra
flea market	mercato delle pulci	mer'kato delle'pultʃi
fortress	fortezza	for'tettsa
fountain	fontana	fon'tana
fun fair	luna park	luna'park
garden	giardino	dʒar'dino
gate	porta	'pɔrta
historical centre	centro storico	'tʃentro 'stɔriko
lakeside	lungolago	lungo'lago
library	biblioteca	bibljo'tɛka
mausoleum	mausoleo	mauzo'lɛo
park	parco	'parko
parliament	parlamento	parla'mento
picture gallery	pinacoteca	pinako'tɛka

SIGHTSEEING AND TOURS 5.2

planetarium	planetario	*plane'tarjo*
quarter	quartiere	*kwar'tjɛre*
ruins	rovine	*ro'vine*
sea front	lungomare	*lungo'mare*
stadium	stadio	*'stadjo*
Stock Exchange	borsa	*'borsa*
temple	tempio	*'tɛmpjo*
theatre	teatro	*te'atro*
tomb	tomba	*'tomba*
tower	torre	*'torre*
town hall	municipio	*muni'tʃipjo*
town walls	mura	*'mura*
university	università	*universi'ta*

Where is the tourist office?
Dov'è l'uffico turistico?

What is there of interest to visit?
Che cosa c'è di interessante da visitare?

Have you got any brochures?
Ha dei pieghevoli illustrativi?

What are the opening times?
Qual è l'orario d'apertura?

Is it open on Sundays?
È aperto la domenica?

How long does it take to visit … ?
Quanto tempo ci vuole per visitare … ?

Is there a guided tour to … ?
C'è una visita guidata a … ?

I'd like a guide in English.
Vorrei una guida in inglese.

What is this building?
Che cos'è questo edificio?

Who was it built by?
Chi l'ha costruito?

5.2 SIGHTSEEING AND TOURS

What period is it from?
A che epoca risale?
Where is the house/birthplace of ... ?
Dov'è la casa (natale) di ... ?
**Are there reduced rates for young people/
old age pensioners/groups?**
Ci sono riduzioni per giovani/pensionati/gruppi?

VISITING MUSEUMS, EXHIBITS AND COLLECTIONS

In the course of a visit, you may find the following signs:

È vietato fotografare.
The taking of photographs is strictly forbidden.
Vietato fotografare col flash.
Use of flash forbidden.
Vietato toccare le opere.
Do not touch the exhibits.
Opera in restauro.
In restoration.
Sala/ala chiusa per restauri.
Room/Wing closed for restoration.
Sale non aperte al pubblico.
Rooms not open to the general public.

Where is ...
Dov'è ...
... the monument to ... ?
... il monumento ... ?
... the museum entrance?
... l'ingresso del museo?
... the ticket office for the ... museum?
... la biglietteria del museo ... ?

Which museum houses the painting/statue by/of ... ?
In quale museo è conservato il quadro/la statua di ... ?

Il museo è chiuso per restauri.
The museum is closed for refurbishment.

How much is the ticket?
Quanto costa il biglietto?
Is there a collective ticket for all the museums in the city/town?
Esiste un biglietto cumulativo per tutti i musei della città?
Is there a period ticket valid for more than one day?
Esistono biglietti validi più giorni?
Is there a day of free entrance?
C'è un giorno in cui l'ingresso è gratuito?
What are the museum opening times?
Che orario fa il museo … ?
When is the closing day?
Qual è il giorno di chiusura?
How long will the exhibition of … last?
Fino a quando dura la mostra di … ?

La mostra è stata prorogata fino al … .
The exhibition has been extended until … .

Where is the cloakroom?
Dov'è il guardaroba?
Are there guided visits in English/Italian?
Ci sono visite guidate in inglese/italiano?
What time does the guided tour start?
A che ora comincia la visita guidata?
Have you got a guide/a catalogue in English/Italian?
Ha una guida/un catalogo in inglese/italiano?
Is there an audioguide?
C'è una audioguida?
Is the … collection open to visitors?
È possibile visitare la collezione … ?

Questa sezione è aperta a giorni alterni.
This section is open on alternate days.

5.2 SIGHTSEEING AND TOURS

Where is the section on/of … ?
Dov'è la sezione di … ?
Where is the room of … ?
Dov'è la sala di … ?
Who painted this picture?
Chi ha dipinto questo quadro?

> **Opera attribuita a … .**
> Work attributed to … .

What period is this work from?
A che epoca risale quest'opera?
Where is …
Dov'è …

> **… the toilet/bar/restaurant?**
> … la toilette/il bar/ristorante?
> **… the lift/staircase/exit?**
> … l'ascensore/la scala/l'uscita?
> **… the book shop?**
> … il book-shop/la libreria?

When does the museum close?
Fra quanto chiude il museo?

> **Il museo chiude fra 30 minuti. Avvicinarsi all'uscita.**
> The museum closes in 30 minutes. Please go to the exit.

STYLES, TECHNIQUES, OBJECTS AND MATERIALS

altar piece	pala	'pala
armoury	armatura	arma'tura
bas-relief	bassorilievo	bassori'ljevo
bronze	bronzo	'brondzo
bust	busto	'busto
canvas	tela	'tela
capital	capitello	kapi'tɛllo
carving	intaglio	in'taʎʎo

ceramics	ceramica	*tʃeˈramika*
column	colonna	*koˈlonna*
copper	rame	*ˈrame*
copy	copia	*ˈkɔpja*
drawing	disegno	*diˈseɲɲo*
earthenware	terracotta	*tɛrraˈkɔtta*
enamel	smalto	*ˈzmalto*
engraving	incisione	*intʃiˈzjone*
etching	acquaforte	*akkwaˈfɔrte*
frame	cornice	*korˈnitʃe*
fresco	affresco	*afˈfresko*
frieze	fregio	*ˈfredʒo*
furniture	mobilio	*moˈbiljo*
glyptic	glittica	*ˈglittika*
graffito	graffito	*grafˈfito*
handicrafts	artigianato	*artidʒaˈnato*
icon	icona	*iˈkona*
inlaid work	intarsio	*inˈtarsjo*
ivory	avorio	*aˈvɔrjo*
landscape	paesaggio	*paeˈzaddʒo*
lithograph	litografia	*litograˈfia*
majolica	maiolica	*maˈjɔlika*
marble	marmo	*ˈmarmo*
medal	medaglia	*meˈdaʎʎa*
miniature	miniatura	*minjaˈtura*
mosaic	mosaico	*moˈzaiko*
mummy	mummia	*ˈmummja*
numismatics	numismatica	*numizˈmatika*
obelisk	obelisco	*obeˈlisko*
oil painting	pittura a olio	*pitˈtura aˈɔljo*
painter	pittore	*pitˈtore*
painting	dipinto	*diˈpinto*
panel	tavola	*ˈtavola*
pastel	pastello	*pasˈtɛllo*
pediment	frontone	*fronˈtone*

5.2 SIGHTSEEING AND TOURS

picture	quadro	'kwadro
plaster	stucco	'stukko
porcelain	porcellana	portʃe'lana
portrait	ritratto	ri'tratto
sarcophagus	sarcofago	sar'kɔfago
sculpture	scultura	skul'tura
self portrait	autoritratto	autori'tratto
serigraph	serigrafia	serigra'fia
silver	argento	ar'dʒento
sketch	bozzetto/ schizzo	bot'tsetto/ 'skittso
spa	terme	'tɛrme
stele	stele	'stɛle
still life	natura morta	na'tura 'mɔrta
tapestry	arazzo	a'rattso
tempera	tempera	'tɛmpera
vase	vaso	'vazo
water colour	acquerello	akkwe'rɛllo
wood	legno	'leɲɲo
woodcut	xilografia	ksilogra'fia

CHURCHES AND PLACES OF WORSHIP

abbey	abbazia	abbat'tsia
altar	altare	al'tare
altar piece	pala	'pala
apsis	abside	'abside
baptistery	battistero	battis'tero
basilica	basilica	ba'zilika
cathedral	cattedrale	katte'drale
cathedral	duomo	'dwɔmo
cemetry	cimitero	tʃimi'tɛro
chapel	cappella	kap'pɛlla
choir	coro	'kɔro
church	chiesa	'kjɛza

cloister	chiostro	'kjɔstro
confessional	confessionale	konfessjo'nale
convent	convento	kon'vɛnto
crucifix	crocifisso	krotʃi'fisso
crypt	cripta	'kripta
dome	cupola	'kupola
facade	facciata	fat'tʃata
font	fonte battesimale	'fonte battezi'male
monastery	monastero	monas'tɛro
mosque	moschea	mos'kɛa
nave/aisle	navata	na'vata
organ	organo	'ɔrgano
portal	portale	por'tale
pulpit	pulpito	'pulpito
relic	reliquia	re'likwja
rosette	rosone	ro'zone
sacristy	sacrestia	sakres'tia
spire	guglia	'guʎʎa
stained-glass window	vetrata	ve'trata
steeple/bell-tower	campanile	kampa'nile
synagogue	sinagoga	sina'gɔga
transept	transetto	tran'sɛtto

Is the church open to tourists?
Si può visitare la chiesa?
When was it built?
Quando è stata costruita?

5.2 SIGHTSEEING AND TOURS

TOURS, EXCURSIONS AND SIDE TRIPS

See also the situation on Travelling on Buses and Coaches, Area 2.5.

Where can I find a tourist agency?
Dov'è un'agenzia turistica?
I'd like to go on …
Vorrei fare …

    … a guided tour of the city.
    … una visita guidata della città.
    … an excursion to … .
    … un'escursione a … .
    … a boat trip to … .
    … una gita in battello a … .

How much does it cost per person?
Quanto costa a persona?
What is included in the price?
Che cosa è compreso nel prezzo?

    Sono compresi: pullman, guida, biglietto d'ingresso, colazione al sacco/in ristorante.
    Included are: coach, guide, entrance ticket, packed lunch/lunch in a restaurant.

How long does it take?
Quanto tempo ci vuole?
What time is the departure/return?
A che ora si parte/si torna?
What is the tour plan?
Qual è il programma della visita?
Are there English-speaking guides?
Ci sono guide che parlano inglese?
Where is the point of departure?
Da dove si parte?
Where is the stop for lunch?
Dove sarà il pranzo?

SIGHTSEEING AND TOURS 5.2

Where is the overnight stop?
Dove pernotteremo?
Are we covered by insurance?
Saremo coperti da assicurazione?

■ CANCELLATIONS AND COMPLAINTS
I'd like to change the excursion date.
Vorrei cambiare la data dell'escursione.
I'd like to cancel my booking.
Vorrei cancellare la prenotazione.
Am I allowed a refund in full?
Ho diritto al rimborso per intero?
You did not keep to the programme.
Non avete rispettato il programma.
In the excursion programme ...
Nel programma dell'escursione ...

    ... there was supposed to be a visit to ... .
    ... era prevista anche la visita di ... .
    ... the price was inclusive of lunch.
    ... il pranzo era incluso nel prezzo.
    ... the price was inclusive of the entrance ticket.
    ... il biglietto era incluso nel prezzo.

AT THE SEASIDE, THE LAKE, THE RIVER

bathing establishment	stabilimento balneare	stabili'mento balne'are
beach towel	telo da spiaggia	'telo das'pjaddʒa
boat	barca	'barka
motorboat	a motore	ammo'tore
rowing boat	a remi	ar'rɛmi
sailing boat	a vela	av'vela
buoy	boa	'bɔa
cabin/hut	cabina	ka'bina
deck chair	sedia a sdraio	'sɛdja az'drajo

203

flippers	pinne	'pinne
life-belt	salvagente	salva'dʒɛnte
life guard	bagnino	baɲ'ɲino
mask	maschera	'maskera
nozzle	boccaglio	bok'kaʎʎo
sea	mare	'mare
calm sea	calmo	'kalmo
choppy sea	mosso	'mɔsso
skiff	canotto	ka'nɔtto
surf board	tavola da surf	'tavola das'sɛrf
windsurf board	da windsurf	dawwin'sɛrf
umbrella	ombrellone	ombrel'lone

Dov'è la spiaggia più vicina?
Where is the nearest beach?
Is it a sandy/pebbly beach?
È una spiaggia sabbiosa/sassosa?
Are there any currents?
Ci sono correnti?
Is it safe to bathe here?
È sicuro fare il bagno qui?
Can I hire the kit for subsea fishing?
È possibile noleggiare l'equipaggiamento per la pesca subacquea?
I'd like to hire ... .
Vorrei noleggiare ... .

> **Divieto di balneazione.**
> No bathing.

OUTDOORS

bridge	ponte	'ponte
canal	canale	ka'nale
cliff	scogliera	skoʎ'ʎɛra
ditch	fossato	fos'sato
dune	duna	'duna
field	campo	'kampo
flora	flora	'flɔra
forest	foresta	fo'rɛsta
hill	collina	kol'lina
lake	lago	'lago
meadow	prato	'prato
moor	brughiera	bru'gjɛra
mountain	montagna	mon'taɲɲa
natural park	parco naturale	'parko natu'rale
path	sentiero	sen'tjɛro
pond	stagno	'staɲɲo
refuge	rifugio	ri'fudʒo
river	fiume	'fjume
spring	sorgente	sord'ʒɛnte
stream	ruscello	ruʃ'ʃɛllo
top	cima	'tʃima
valley	valle	'valle
waterfall	cascata	kas'kata
wildlife	fauna	'fauna
wood	bosco	'bɔsko

Is it a panoramic road?
È una strada panoramica?
Is it a nature trail?
È un itinerario naturalistico?
Are there guided tours of the park?
Ci sono visite guidate del parco?

5.2 SIGHTSEEING AND TOURS

Are there any villages in the vicinity?
Ci sono villaggi nelle vicinanze?
Can we get there on foot/on horseback/by bicycle?
Ci si può arrivare /a piedi/a cavallo/in bicicletta?
Have you got a map ...
Avete una cartina ...
>   **... of itineraries?**
>   ... degli itinerari?
>   **... of paths?**
>   ... dei sentieri?

■ SIGNS YOU MAY SEE DURING YOUR EXCURSION

>   **Vietato raccogliere fiori.**
>   Do not pick the flowers.
>   **Non abbandonare i sentieri.**
>   Do not leave the paths.
>   **Non date da mangiare agli animali.**
>   Do not feed the animals.
>   **Pericolo. Vietato scendere dall'automobile.**
>   Danger. Do not leave your vehicle.

CINEMA, THEATRE, CONCERTS

■ PROGRAMS AND TICKETS

act	tempo	'tɛmpo
auditoriums	multisala	multi'sala
ballet	balletto	bal'letto
box seats	palchetto	'palketto
choreography	coreografia	koreogra'fia
circus	circo	'tʃirko
company	compagnia	kompaɲ'ɲia
dancing	danza	'dandza
classical ballet	classica	'klassika
folk dance	folkloristica	folklo'ristika
modern dance	moderna	mo'dɛrna
direction/ production	regia	re'dʒia
dramatic play	dramma	'dramma
evening	serata	se'rata
gala evening	di gala	di'gala
exhibition	esibizione/ rassegna	ezibit'tsjone/ ras'seɲɲa
first night	prima	'prima
gallery	galleria	galle'ria
hall	sala	'sala
interval	intervallo	inter'vallo
mime	mimo	'mimo
movie	film	film
music	musica	'muzika
chamber m.	da camera	dak'kamera
operatic m.	lirica	'lirika
sacred m.	sacra	'sakra
symphonic m.	sinfonica	sin'fonika
traditional folk m.	tradizionale	tradittsjo'nale
opera	opera	'ɔpera
oratorio	oratorio	ora'tɔrjo

5.3 ENTERTAINMENT AND LEISURE

performance charity performance	rappresentazione di beneficenza	_rapprezentat'tsjone dibenefi'tʃɛntsa_
play	commedia	_kom'mɛdja_
preview	anteprima	_ante'prima_
programme	programma	_pro'gramma_
puppets	marionette	_marjo'nette_
repeat	replica	_'rɛplika_
scene	scena	_'ʃɛna_
scenery	scenografia	_ʃenogra'fia_
screen	schermo	_'skɛrmo_
screening	proiezione	_projet'tsjone_
seat	poltrona	_pol'trona_
show matinée children's show	spettacolo diurno per bambini	_spet'takolo 'djurno perbam'bini_
son et lumière	suoni e luci	_'swɔni el'lutʃi_
orchestra (seating)	platea	_pla'tɛa_
usher(ette)	maschera	_'maskera_
variety	varietà	_varje'ta_

■ SIGNS YOU MAY SEE OR ANNOUNCEMENTS YOU MAY HEAR
AT THE THEATRE

> **Vietato ai minori di ... anni.**
> No admittance to minors of ... years.
> **Rappresentazione annullata/rinviata al ... .**
> Performance cancelled/postponed to ... .

Have you got this evening's cinema programme, please?
Ha il programma dei cinema di stasera?
Have you got the weekly theatre programme?
Ha il programma settimanale dei teatri?
I'd like the ... festival programme.
Vorrei il programma del festival di ... .

Have you got a list of entertainments, please?
C'è un bollettino con il programma degli spettacoli?
Must one book seats beforehand?
È necessario prenotare il posto?
Where can I get tickets for ... ?
Dove posso trovare i biglietti per ... ?

> **Direttamente al botteghino del teatro.**
> At the theatre box office.
> **La prevendita è in ... .**
> The advance ticket office is in ... .

How much is a seat in the stalls/in the dress circle/in the gallery/in a box?
Quanto costa un posto in platea/in prima/seconda galleria/in un palco?
I'd like to book ... seats in ... for the concert of ... .
Vorrei prenotare ... biglietti in ... per il concerto di ... .

> **In quella data è tutto esaurito.**
> Tickets for that date are all sold out.
> **Sono rimasti posti solo per il giorno ... .**
> There are still tickets just for ...

Are these seats good?
Sono buoni questi posti?
I'd like a central seat.
Vorrei un posto centrale.
What time does the show begin/end?
A che ora inizia/termina lo spettacolo?

5.3 ENTERTAINMENT AND LEISURE

■ INFORMATION ON SHOWS

Can you suggest a good ... music concert?
Può consigliarmi un buon concerto di musica ... ?
What kind is it?
Che genere è?
Who is/are ...
Chi è/sono ...

    ... the author/the play producer/the film director/the leading actors?
    ... l'autore/il regista/gli attori principali?
    ... the conductor/the soloist?
    ... il direttore d'orchestra/ il solista?
    ... the orchestra/the dancers?
    ... l'orchestra/i ballerini?

Is it in ... [language]?
È in ... ?
Are there any sub-titles?
Ci sono sottititoli?

■ INSIDE THE THEATRE

Where is the cloakroom/the toilet?
Dov'è il guardaroba/la toilette?
Where are these seats?
Dove sono questi posti?
Can I change my seat? I cannot see/hear anything!
È possibile cambiare posto? Non vedo/sento niente!

> **Lo spettacolo è già iniziato,**
> **non può entrare in sala.**
> The performance has already begun.
> You can't go into the auditorium.

Is there an interval?
C'è l'intervallo?
Where can I get a refund for my ticket?
Dove rimborsano i biglietti?

NIGHT CLUBS AND DISCOTHÈQUES

Could you suggest …
Può consigliarmi …

> **… a piano bar/night club/discotheque?**
> … un pianobar/night-club/una discoteca?
> **… somewhere where … music is played?**
> … un locale dove suonano musica … ?

What time does it close?
A che ora chiude il locale?
What kind of place is it?
Che genere di locale è?

■ **DRESSING APPROPRIATELY**
To enter some clubs, restaurants and theatres, appropriate attire is required.

> **È richiesto/a l'abito da sera/giacca e cravatta/l'abito lungo.**
> Evening dress/jacket and tie/formal dress is requested.

5.3 ENTERTAINMENT AND LEISURE

SPORTS AND SPORTING EVENTS

athletics	atletica	a'tlɛtika
basket ball	pallacanestro	pallaka'nɛstro
boxing	pugilato	pudʒi'lato
canoeing	canottaggio	kanot'taddʒo
competitor (racing)	corridore	korri'dore
cross-country	fondo	'fondo
cycling	ciclismo	tʃi'klizmo
fault/foul	fallo	'fallo
fencing	scherma	'skɛrma
finals	finale	fi'nale
finishing post	traguardo	tra'gwardo
friendly	amichevole	ami'kevole
goal	rete	'rete
gymnastics	ginnastica	dʒin'nastika
heat	batteria	batte'ria
martial arts	arti marziali	'arti mar'tsjali
match	incontro	in'kontro
middle-ground racing	mezzofondo	mɛddzo'fondo
net (tennis, volleyball)	rete	'rete
player	giocatore	dʒoka'tore
playing field/ court/course	campo di gioco	'kampo di'dʒɔko
quarter finals	quarti di finale	'kwarti difi'nale
race course	ippodromo	ip'pɔdromo
race car driver	pilota	pi'lɔta
racing	corsa	'korsa
foot	podistica	po'distika
greyhound	di cani	di'kani
horse racing	di cavalli	dika'valli
motorcar	automobilistica	automobi'listika
motorcycle	motociclistica	mototʃi'klistika

ping-pong	ping-pong	pim'pɔŋ
rock climbing	alpinismo	alpi'nizmo
sailing	vela	'vela
sailplaning	volo a vela	'volo av'vela
shot/throw	tiro	'tiro
archery	con l'arco	kon'larko
clay-pigeon shooting	al piattello	alpjat'tɛllo
sky diving	parapendio	parapen'dio
touring by bicycle	cicloturismo	tʃiklotu'rizmo
water skiing	sci nautico	ʃin'nautiko

What sports facilities are there here?
Quali sport si possono praticare qui?
Where can you play a game of … ?
Dove si può fare una partita a … ?
Where can I find …
Dove si trova …

… a(n) open-air/covered swimming pool?
… una piscina all'aperto/al chiuso?
… a tennis court/golf course?
… un campo da tennis/da golf?
… a riding stable?
… un maneggio?
I'd like to take … lessons.
Vorrei prendere delle lezioni di … .
I am a beginner. I have never played … .
Sono principiante, non ho mai giocato a … .
I play … quite well.
Gioco abbastanza bene a … .
I am looking for someone to play … with.
Cerco qualcuno con cui giocare a … .
I'd like to book a court for tomorrow from … to … .
Vorrei prenotare il campo per domani dalle … alle … .

5.3 ENTERTAINMENT AND LEISURE

È riservato ai soci/ai clienti dell'hotel.
Reserved for members/hotel clients.

I'd like to hire ...
Vorrei noleggiare ...
... a fishing rod.
... una canna da pesca.
... a tennis racket.
... una racchetta da tennis.
... a pair of skates.
... un paio di pattini.
... a windsurfing board/yacht.
... un windsurf/una barca a vela.
Is the water in the swimming pool heated?
L'acqua della piscina è riscaldata?

Per entrare in piscina è obbligatorio l'uso della cuffia.
Swimming caps must be worn in the pool.
Obbligo di fare la doccia prima di entrare in piscina.
Showers are compulsory before entering the pool.
Non fare tuffi.
No diving.

Is it an open-air court?
Il campo è all'aperto?
Is there any fishing here?
È possibile pescare qui?
Is skin diving practised here?
È possibile fare immersioni subacquee?
Is there any underwater fishing here?
È possibile fare pesca subacquea?

Sì, ma senza bombole di ossigeno.
Yes, but without air cylinders.

ENTERTAINMENT AND LEISURE 5.3

■ WINTER SPORTS

boots/shoes	scarponi	skar'poni
cable car	ovovia	ɔvo'via
chair lift	seggiovia	seddʒo'via
ice skates	pattini da ghiaccio	'pattini dag'gjattʃo
ski lift	sciovia	ʃio'via
skiing	sci	ʃi
downhill	da discesa	daddiʃ'ʃesa
cross-country	da fondo	daf'fondo
sticks	bastoncini	baston'tʃini

Where do I get a skipass?
Dove si fa lo skipass?
Where are the ski runs?
Dove sono le piste da sci?
Where is the ski school?
Dov'è la scuola di sci?
I'd like to take skiing lessons.
Vorrei prendere delle lezioni di sci.
I am a beginner.
Sono principiante.
I'd like to hire … .
Vorrei noleggiare … .
Where is the cableway?
Dov'è la funivia?
Is this ski run difficult?
È difficile questa pista?

■ SIGNS YOU MAY SEE ON THE SKI-RUNS

Non lasciare la pista.
Do not ski off the track.
Pericolo valanghe.
Danger of avalanches.

5.3 ENTERTAINMENT AND LEISURE

CARDS AND GAMES

ace	asso	'asso
balls	boccette	bot'tʃette
bet	puntare	pun'tare
bid	dichiarare	dikja'rare
billiards	biliardo	bi'ljardo
bishop	alfiere	al'fjɛre
canasta	canasta	ka'nasta
casino	casinò	kasi'nɔ
checkmate	scacco matto	'skakko 'matto
chess	scacchi	'skakki
chessboard	scacchiera	skak'kjɛra
clubs	fiori	'fjori
cue	stecca	'stekka
cut	taglio	'taʎʎo
deal	distribuire	distribu'ire
diamonds	quadri	'kwadri
dice	dadi	'dadi
draughts/checkers	dama	'dama
game	gioco	'dʒɔko
game of skill	d'abilità	dabili'ta
game of cards	di carte	di'karte
games table	tavolo	'tavolo
	da gioco	dad'dʒɔko
hearts	cuori	'kwɔri
jack	fante	'fante
joker	jolly	'dʒɔlli
king, queen	re/regina	re/re'dʒina
knight	cavallo	ka'vallo
object ball/jack	pallino	pal'lino
pack	mazzo	'mattso
pair	coppia	'kɔppja
partner	compagno	kom'paɲɲo
pass	passare	pas'sare

ENTERTAINMENT AND LEISURE 5.3

pawn	pedone	pe'done
piece/chessman	pedina	pe'dina
playing cards	carte	'karte
points	punti	'punti
queen	donna	'dɔnna
rook	torre	'torre
run	scala	'skala
skittles	birilli	bi'rilli
spades	picche	'pikke
suit/ flush (poker)	colore	ko'lore
the king in check	scacco al re	'skakko al're
three	tris	tris
turn/move	mossa	'mɔssa
two pairs	doppia coppia	'doppja 'kɔppja

Where can I play … ?
Dove posso giocare a … ?
Where can I buy counters?
Dove si comprano i gettoni?
Have you got any party games?
Avete giochi di società?
I'd like to enter for the … tournament.
Vorrei iscrivermi al torneo di … .
Where can I find a gaming room/casino?
Dove si trova una sala giochi/il casinò?
What are the minimum stakes?
Qual è la puntata minima?
Could you explain the game to me, please?
Può spiegarmi il gioco?
What is the resort's entertainment programme … ?
Qual è il programma delle attività del villaggio per … ?
Where do I sign up for the … tournament/course?
Dove posso iscrivermi al torneo/corso di … ?

5.3 ENTERTAINMENT AND LEISURE

Where can I hire … equipment?
Dove posso noleggiare l'attrezzatura per … ?
Shall we have a game of … ?
Vogliamo fare una partita a … ?
I would like to play but I have no partner.
Vorrei giocare ma non ho un compagno.
I can't play … .
Non so giocare a … .
I don't like gambling.
Non amo giocare d'azzardo.
I don't want to bet.
Non voglio giocare di soldi.
Who counts the points?
Chi tiene il punteggio?

LOOKING FOR A SHOP, AN OBJECT, A SERVICE

This list contains those articles which are not mentioned in the specific sections that follow.

addresses	recapiti	re'kapiti
antiques	antiquario	anti'kwarjo
auctions	aste	'aste
bakery	panetteria	panette'ria
bicycle	biciclette	bitʃi'klette
(repairs)	(riparazione)	riparat'tsjone
bookshop	libreria	libre'ria
carpets	tappeti	tap'peti
ceramics	ceramiche	tʃe'ramike
china (shop)	porcellane	portʃel'lane
crystalware	cristalleria	kristalle'ria
dairy	latteria/formaggi	latte'ria/for'maddʒi
delicatessen	gastronomia	gastrono'mia
dress maker's/ tailor	sartoria	sarto'ria
electrician	elettricista	elettri'tʃista
embroidery	ricami	ri'kami
fancy glassware	vetri artistici	'vetri ar'tistitʃi
fancy goods	bigiotteria	bidʒotte'ria
fishmongery	pescheria	peske'ria
furnishings	arredamento	arreda'mento
furniture	mobili	'mɔbili
furrier's	pellicceria	pellittʃe'ria
greengrocery	frutta e verdura	'frutta evver'dura
grocer's	salumeria/ drogheria/ alimentari	salume'ria/ droge'ria/ alimen'tari
haberdashery	merceria	mertʃe'ria
hardware store	ferramenta	ferra'menta
health food	erboristeria	erboriste'ria

hunting equipment	armeria	*arme'ria*
ice-cream parlour	gelateria	*dʒelate'ria*
instruments	strumenti	*stru'menti*
items	articoli	*ar'tikoli*
camping items	da campeggio	*dakkam'peddʒo*
gift items	da regalo	*darre'galo*
travel items	da viaggio	*davvi'addʒo*
ecclesiastic i.	religiosi	*reli'dʒosi*
sports items	sportivi	*spor'tivi*
light fittings	illuminazione	*illuminat'tsjone*
maternity wear	premaman	*prema'man*
and infant care	e neonati	*enneo'nati*
pastry shop	pasticceria	*pastittʃe'ria*
pets	animali	*ani'mali*
posters	manifesti	*mani'festi*
prints, engravings	stampe/incisioni	*'stampe/intʃi'zjoni*
rotisserie	rosticceria	*rostittʃe'ria*
souvenirs	souvenir	*suve'nir*
stamp collecting	filatelia	*filate'lia*
stereo and	stereofonia	*stereofo'nia*
hi-fi	e alta fedeltà	*e'alta fedel'ta*
toys	giocattoli	*dʒo'kattoli*
veterinary surgeon	veterinario	*veteri'narjo*
wines and liqueurs	vini e liquori	*'vini elli'kwori*

Where can I find ...
Dove si trova ...

    ... the nearest ... shop?
    ... il più vicino negozio di ... ?
    ... a shopping centre/a department store?
    ... un centro commerciale/un grande magazzino?
    ... a supermarket/a market?
    ... un supermercato/un mercato?

What are the opening times? What are the closing days?
Che orario fa? Quali sono i giorni di chiusura?
Can you tell me where there is a good shopping area?
Può indicarmi una zona con dei buoni negozi?
Could you suggest ...
Può consigliarmi ...

... a good ... (shop)?
... un buon negozio di ... ?
... a ... (shop) which is not too expensive/not touristy?
... un negozio di ... non troppo caro/non turistico?

IN THE SHOP

The following signs may be posted in a shop window:

Ingresso libero
Free entrance
Prezzi fissi
Fixed prices
Servitevi da soli e pagate alla cassa.
Self service. Please pay at the cash desk.

■ WATCH FOR SIGNS THAT SAY:

Liquidazione/Sconti/Saldi
Sales/Discounts/Sales
Vendita promozionale/Offerta speciale/Occasioni
Promotional sales/Special offers/Bargains

cashier	cassiere/a	kas'sjɛre/kas'sjɛra
department	reparto	re'parto
goods	merce	'mɛrtʃe
shop assistant	commesso/a	kom'messo/ kom'messa

Desidera? Posso aiutarla?
Can I help you? Do you need any help?

5.4 SHOPPING

I'd like to have a look.
Vorrei dare un'occhiata.
I'd like to see that ... in the window/on the counter/on the shelf.
Vorrei vedere quel/quella ... in vetrina/sul banco/sullo scaffale.

> **Non è in vendita.**
> It's not for sale.
> **Quale colore preferisce?**
> Which colour do you prefer?

Have you got ...
Avete ...
> **... any other brands/any other colours/any other models?**
> ... altre marche/altri colori/altri modelli?
> **... something ...**
> ... qualcosa di ...
> **... different/better/cheaper?**
> ... diverso/meglio/meno caro?
> **... lighter/darker?**
> ... più chiaro/scuro?
> **... bigger/smaller?**
> ... più grande/piccolo?
> **... lighter/heavier(thicker)?**
> ... più leggero/pesante?
> **... more up-to-date/typical?**
> ... più recente/tipico?

> **È esaurito, arriverà fra ... giorni.**
> It is sold out. New stocks will arrive in ... days.

Could you order it, please? I need it by ... .
Può ordinarlo? Mi occorre entro ... .

DEPARTMENT STORES, SUPERMARKETS AND SHOPPING CENTRES

To find your bearings in a department store or a shopping centre, watch for signs. To find the exact article you are looking for, refer to the list of shops and products posted at the entrance or ask at the Centre's information desk.

Where are the trolleys/shopping carts?
Dove sono i carrelli?
Where is the ... department?
Dov'è il reparto ... ?
Is there a map of the shopping centre?
Esiste una piantina del centro?
Where is ...
Dov'è ...

    ... the lift/the escalator/the exit?
    ... l'ascensore/la scala mobile/l'uscita?
    ... the cash desk/customer services office?
    ... la cassa/l'ufficio reclami e cambi?

■ **FABRICS**

acrylic	acrilico	a'kriliko
batiste	batista	ba'tista
camelhair	pelo di cammello	'pelo dikam'mɛllo
canvas	tela	'tela
cashmere	cachemere	'kaʃmir
corduroy	velluto a coste	vel'luto ak'kɔste
cotton	cotone	ko'tone
elasticized	elasticizzato	elastitʃid'dʒato
felt	feltro	'feltro
flannel	flanella	fla'nɛlla
gabardine	gabardina	gabar'dina
linen	lino	'lino
muslin	mussolina	musso'lina

225

5.4 SHOPPING

pattern	disegno	di'seɲɲo
polka dot	a pois	a'pwa
checked	a quadretti	akkwa'dretti
striped	a righe	ar'rige
patterned	fantasia	fanta'zia
tartan	scozzese	skot'tsese
remnant	scampolo	'skampolo
satin	raso	'razo
shetland wool	shetland	'ʃetland
silk	seta	'seta
synthetic fibre	fibra sintetica	'fibra sin'tɛtika
taffeta	taffetà	taffe'ta
towelling	spugna	'spuɲɲa
tulle	tulle	'tulle
unshrinkable	irrestringibile	irrestrin'dʒibile
velvet	velluto	vel'luto
wool	lana	'lana

Is this fabric hand-woven?
È un tessuto fatto a mano?
What is the width of the rolls?
Di che altezza sono le pezze?
Have you got it in a plain colour?
Lo avete in tinta unita?
How much is it the metre?
Quanto viene al metro?

> **Misto lino 60%/fibra sintetica 40%.**
> Mixture 60% linen/40% synthetic fibre.

CLOTHING

apron	grembiule	*grem'bjule*
bathing costume	costume da bagno	*kos'tume dab'baɲɲo*
blouse	camicetta	*kami'tʃetta*
coat	cappotto	*kap'pɔtto*
double-breasted (jacket)	doppiopetto	*doppjo'pɛtto*
dress	abito	*'abito*
fur	pelliccia	*pel'littʃa*
hood	cappuccio	*kap'puttʃo*
jacket	giacca	*'dʒakka*
jersey	maglia	*'maʎʎa*
jumper/sweater	golf	*gɔlf*
neck line	scollatura	*skolla'tura*
plush sweater	felpa	*'felpa*
pullover (thick)	maglione	*maʎ'ʎone*
raincoat	impermeabile	*imperme'abile*
shirt	camicia	*ka'mitʃa*
shorts	pantaloncini	*pantalon'tʃini*
skirt	gonna	*'gɔnna*
sports jacket	giubbotto	*dʒub'bɔtto*
suit	vestito	*ves'tito*
suit (ladies)	tailleur	*ta'jœr*
trousers	pantaloni	*panta'loni*
vest	canottiera/ maglietta	*kanot'tjɛra/ maʎ'ʎetta*
waistcoat	gilet	*dʒi'lɛ*
wind-cheater	giacca a vento	*'dʒakka av'vɛnto*

I'd like a … .
Vorrei un … .
I'd like a … for my son/daughter.
Vorrei un … per mio/a figlio/a.

5.4 SHOPPING

Che taglia porta?
What size are you/is he/she?

I am/He is/She is British size … .
Porto/a la taglia … inglese.
Have you got any other colours?
Avete altri colori?
I'd like a colour that matches this.
Vorrei un colore che si intoni con questo.
Can I try it on?
Posso provarlo?

Si accomodi nel camerino di prova.
The fitting booth is over there.
Come le sta?
How does it fit?

It's all right.
Va bene.
It's a little too …
È un po' …
… tight/big.
… stretto/largo.
… long/short.
… lungo/corto.
… ample/close-fitting.
… abbondante/aderente.
I'd like a bigger/smaller size.
Vorrei la taglia superiore/inferiore.
What material is it?
Che tessuto è?
Could you make some alterations?
Potete fare delle modifiche?
Could you do the hem?
Potete fare l'orlo?
How long will it take?
Quanto tempo ci vuole?

SEWING ITEMS

needle	ago	'ago
pin	spillo	'spillo
press stud/ snap	automatico	auto'matiko
safety pin	spillo di sicurezza	'spillo disiku'rettsa
thimble	ditale	di'tale
thread	filo	'filo

UNDERGARMENTS

brassière	reggiseno	reddʒi'seno
dress slip	sottoveste	sotto'vɛste
dressing gown	vestaglia	ves'taʎʎa
garter	giarrettiere	dʒarret'tjɛre
girdle	guaina	'gwaina
lingerie/ underwear	biancheria	bjanke'ria
night dress	camicia da notte	ka'mitʃa dan'nɔtte
pyjamas	pigiama	pi'dʒama
socks	calzini	kal'tsini
stockings	calze	'kaltse
suspender belt	reggicalze	reddʒi'kaltse
tights	calzamaglia	kaltsa'maʎʎa
towelling wrap	accappatoio	akkappa'tojo
underpants/ panties	mutande	mu'tande
waist slip	sottogonna	sotto'gɔnna

HATS, TIES AND ACCESSORIES

bowtie	farfalla	far'falla
braces	bretelle	bre'tɛlle
buckle	fibbia	'fibbja

5.4 SHOPPING

buttons	bottoni	*bot'toni*
cap	berretto	*ber'retto*
cufflinks	gemelli	*dʒe'mɛlli*
hat	cappello	*kap'pɛllo*
scarf	sciarpa	*'ʃarpa*
shawl	scialle	*'ʃalle*
skull cap	papalina	*papa'lina*
tie	cravatta	*kra'vatta*
umbrella	ombrello	*om'brɛllo*

LEATHER GOODS AND BAGGAGE

bag	borsa	*'borsa*
belt	cintura	*tʃin'tura*
chamois leather	camoscio	*ka'mɔʃʃo*
coin purse	portamonete	*portamo'nete*
deerskin	cervo	*'tʃɛrvo*
doeskin	daino	*'daino*
gloves	guanti	*'gwanti*
keyring	portachiavi	*porta'kjavi*
leather	pelle	*'pɛlle*
pigskin	cinghiale	*tʃin'gjale*
purse	borsetta	*bor'setta*
reindeer leather	renna	*'rɛnna*
suede	pelle scamosciata	*'pɛlle skamoʃ'ʃata*
suitcase	valigia	*va'lidʒa*
wallet	portafogli	*porta'fɔʎʎi*

SHOES AND SHOE REPAIR

ballet shoes	ballerine	*balle'rine*
boots	stivali/etti	*sti'vali/stiva'letti*
calf	vitello	*vi'tɛllo*
canvas	tela	*'tela*
clogs	zoccoli	*'tsɔkkoli*

cowhide	vacchetta	vak'ketta
gym shoes	scarpe	'skarpe
	da ginnastica	daddʒin'nastika
kid	capretto	ka'pretto
moccasins	mocassini	mokas'sini
overshoes	soprascarpe	sopras'karpe
patent leather	vernice	ver'nitʃe
sandals	sandali	'sandali
slippers	pantofole	pan'tɔfole
sole	suola	'swɔla
rope sole	di corda	di'kɔrda
leather sole	di cuoio	di'kwɔjo
rubber sole	di gomma	di'gomma
grip sole	di para	di'para
supple leather	cuoio grasso	'kwɔjo 'grasso
upper	tomaia	to'maja
work boots	scarponi	skar'poni

I'd like to try on those shoes in the window.
Vorrei provare quelle scarpe in vetrina.
I'd like a pair of comfortable/elegant/hard-wearing shoes.
Vorrei un paio di scarpe comode/eleganti/robuste.
I'd like them with a high/low heel.
Le vorrei con il tacco alto/basso.
I am English size … .
Porto il … inglese.
They are too narrow/wide.
Sono strette/larghe.
They hurt me.
Mi fanno male.
I'd like to try a bigger/smaller size.
Vorrei provare la misura sopra/sotto.
Have you got the same model with a broader/narrower mould?
Ha lo stesso modello su una forma più larga/stretta?

Have you got any half sizes?
Avete le mezze misure?
Have you got any other colours?
Ha anche altri colori?
Is it real leather?
È vero cuoio?
I'd like some shoe polish/some shoelaces, please.
Vorrei del lucido da scarpe/dei lacci.
Can you shine/sew up/repair/put new soles on my shoes for me?
Può lucidarmi/ricucirmi/ripararmi/risuolarmi le scarpe?
I'd like them reheeled, please.
Vorrei rifare i tacchi.
When will they be ready?
Quando saranno pronte?

FOOD STUFFS

Warning: In Italy food products must be marked with the best before date as well as an expiry date.

Da consumarsi preferibilmente entro il … .
Best before … .
Scade il … .
Expiry date …

Furthermore, some products may have important recommendations such as the following:

Conservare in frigorifero.
Store in the refrigerator.
Prodotto da consumarsi entro … giorni dall'apertura.
Consume within … days after opening.
Non scongelare prima dell'uso.
Do not thaw before use.

Below, we list some expressions regarding the preparation, packing and presentation of food products, some of which are present on labels so that you might establish whether a product suits your needs. For a list of foods and drinks, refer to the vocabulary in the situations on food in Area 3, where you can find various cuts of meat, etc. For weights and measurements, refer to Area 1.

coffee	caffè	kaf'fɛ
coffee beans	in grani	in'grani
ground coffee	macinato	matʃi'nato
packaged c.	confezionato	konfettsjo'nato
dried	essiccato	essik'kato
flour	farina	fa'rina
wheat flour	di grano	di'grano
maize flour	di mais	di'mais
soya flour	di soia	di'sɔja
wholemeal flour	integrale	inte'grale

5.4 SHOPPING

freeze-dried	liofilizzato	ljofilid'dzato
frozen	surgelato	surdʒe'lato
jar	barattolo	ba'rattolo
milk	latte	'latte
full cream	intero	in'tero
pasteurized	pastorizzato	pastorid'dzato
semi-skinned	parzialmente	partsjal'mente
	scremato	skre'mato
skimmed	scremato	skre'mato
long life	UTH	utti'akka
natural flavouring	aromi naturali	a'rɔmi natu'rali
pre-cooked	precotto	pre'kɔtto
preservatives/	conservanti/	konser'vanti/
no preservatives	senza conservanti	'sɛntsa konser'vanti
salted	sotto sale	sotto'sale
slice	fetta	'fetta
stockcubes	dadi per brodo	'dadi per'brɔdo
tin	scatoletta	skato'letta
unpackaged	sfuso	'sfuzo
vacuum-packed	sotto vuoto	sotto'vwɔto
yeast	lievito	'ljɛvito
baking powder	lievito chimico	'ljɛvito 'kimiko

Where is there a …
Dove si trova un negozio …

    … grocer's/butcher's?
    … di alimentari/di macelleria?
    … gourmet shop?
    … di specialità gastronomiche?
    … shop selling diabetic and dietetical products?
    … di prodotti dietetici e per diabetici?
How much is a kilo of … ?
Quanto costa un chilo di … ?
I'd like …
Vorrei …

... some bread.
... del pane.
... two beefsteaks.
... due bistecche di manzo.
... half a kilo of veal cutlets.
... mezzo chilo di fettine di vitella.
... a tin of peeled tomatoes.
... un barattolo di pelati.
... a kilo of potatoes.
... un chilo di patate.
... a hundred grammes of ham.
... un etto di prosciutto.
... a litre of milk.
... un litro di latte.
... a jar of marmalade/jam.
... un vasetto di marmellata.
... a bottle of beer.
... una bottiglia di birra.
... a thin/thick rasher of bacon.
... una fetta sottile/spessa di pancetta.
... a portion of omelette.
... una porzione di frittata.
... a tin of tuna fish.
... una scatoletta di tonno.

Basta così?
Is that everything?
L'abbiamo terminato.
We are out of it.
Vuole altro?
Do you want anything else?

Do you do sandwiches?
Fate panini?
A sandwich with ... .
Un panino con ... .

5.4 SHOPPING

Is it fresh?
È fresco?
Can I help myself?
Posso servirmi da solo?
Would you give me a bag, please?
Mi dà un sacchetto?

HOUSEHOLD ITEMS

alarm clock	sveglia	'zveʎʎa
baking pan	teglia	'teʎʎa
bottle opener	apribottiglie	apribot'tiʎʎe
broom	scopa	'skopa
bucket	secchio	'sekkjo
candle	candele	kan'dele
clothes pegs	mollette	mol'lette
	da bucato	dabbu'kato
colander for pasta	scolapasta	skola'pasta
cork/cap	tappo	'tappo
corkscrew	cavatappi	kava'tappi
deck chair	sedia a sdraio	'sɛdja az'drajo
detergent	detersivo	deter'sivo
laundry	da bucato	dabbu'kato
dishwasher	da lavastoviglie	dallavasto'viʎʎe
automatic	da lavatrice	dallava'tritʃe
dish soap	da piatti	dap'pjatti
dustbin	pattumiera	pattu'mjɛra
dustpan	paletta	pa'letta
	per la spazzatura	perlaspattsa'tura
floor cloth	straccio	'strattʃo
	per pavimenti	perpavi'menti
frying pan	padella	pa'dɛlla
gas-lighter	accendigas	attʃɛndi'gas
grater	grattugia	grat'tudʒa
hammer	martello	mar'tɛllo

236

household matches	fiammiferi da cucina	fjam'miferi dakku'tʃina
insulating tape	nastro isolante	'nastro izo'lante
knife	coltello	kol'tɛllo
nail	chiodo	'kjɔdo
paper glasses	bicchieri di carta	bik'kjɛri di'karta
paper napkins	tovaglioli di carta	tovaʎ'ʎɔli di'karta
paper plates	piatti di carta	'pjatti di'karta
pen-knife	temperino	tempe'rino
plastic cups	bicchieri di plastica	bik'kjɛri di'plastika
plastic gloves	guanti di plastica	'gwanti di'plastika
pliers	tenaglie	te'naʎʎe
rubbish bags	sacchetti per la spazzatura	sak'ketti perlaspattsa'tura
scissors	forbici	'fɔrbitʃi
screwdriver	cacciavite	kattʃa'vite
screws	viti	'viti
sticky tape	nastro adesivo	'nastro ade'zivo
thermos flask	thermos	'tɛrmos
tin opener	apriscatole	apris'katole
toolbox	cassetta degli attrezzi	kas'setta deʎʎat'trettsi

237

ELECTRICITY AND ELECTRICAL APPLIANCES

aerial	antenna	*an'tenna*
battery	batteria	*batte'ria*
blender	frullatore	*frulla'tore*
calculator	calcolatrice	*kalkola'tritʃe*
cassette recorder	registratore	*redʒistra'tore*
dishwasher	lavastoviglie	*lavasto'viʎʎe*
electric plug	spina	*'spina*
eletric razor	rasoio elettrico	*ra'sojo e'lɛttriko*
extension lead	prolunga	*pro'lunga*
iron (travelling)	ferro da stiro	*'fɛrro das'tiro*
	portatile	*por'tatile*
lamp	lampada	*'lampada*
light bulb	lampadina	*lampa'dina*
microwave oven	forno	*'forno*
	a microonde	*ammikro'onde*
multiple socket	presa multipla	*'presa 'multipla*
radio alarm clock	radiosveglia	*radjoz've ʎ ʎa*
refrigerator	frigorifero	*frigo'rifero*
television set	televisore	*televi'zore*
colour	a colori	*akko'lori*
black	in bianco	*im'bjanko*
and white	e nero	*en'nero*
portable	portatile	*por'tatile*
toaster	tostapane	*tosta'pane*
vacuum cleaner	aspirapolvere	*aspira'polvere*
videocamera	videocamera	*video'kamera*
videocassette	videocassetta	*videokas'setta*
videogame	videogioco	*video'dʒɔko*
videorecorder	videoregistratore	*videoredʒistra'tore*
washing machine	lavatrice	*lava'tritʃe*

MUSIC, STEREO AND HI-FI

amplifier	amplificatore	*amplifika'tore*
car radio	autoradio	*auto'radjo*
cassette	cassetta	*kas'setta*
CD player	lettore di CD	*let'tore ditʃid'di*
portable radio	radio portatile	*'radjo por'tatile*
record	disco	*'disko*
record player	giradischi	*dʒira'diski*
recorder	registratore	*redʒistra'tore*
stereo loudspeak- ers/earphones	casse/cuffie stereofoniche	*'kassa/'kuffje stereo'fɔnike*
stereo	stereo	*'stɛreo*

I'd like ... batteries like these.
Vorrei ... pile come queste.
How does it work?
Come funziona?
How long is the guarantee for?
Quanto dura la garanzia?
What is the voltage? Do I need a transformer?
Qual è il voltaggio? È necessario un trasformatore?
I'd like an adaptor for an English plug.
Vorrei un adattatore per una spina inglese.
Can you suggest a radio and TV repairers?
Può indicarmi un riparatore radio-TV?
I think this ... is broken. Could you repair it?
Credo che questo ... sia rotto, può ripararlo?
It is under warranty.
È in garanzia.

> **Non si può riparare.**
> It cannot be repaired.
> **Non le conviene ripararlo, perché spenderà ... .**
> It's not worth repairing it, because it will cost ... .

5.4 SHOPPING

Sarà pronto per venerdì.
It will be ready on Friday.

Have you got any classical/folk/pop/jazz music records/cassettes?
Avete dei dischi/delle cassette di musica classica/folk/leggera/jazz?

Where can I find a bookshop?
Dove si trova una libreria?
Can you tell me where there is a shop for prints and engravings?
Può indicarmi un negozio di stampe e incisioni?
Do you know an antiquarian bookshop?
Conosce una libreria antiquaria?
I'd like a road map of ... .
Vorrei la carta automobilistica di ... .
I'd like a map of ... .
Vorrei la cartina di ... .
I'd like a tourist guide to ... in English.
Vorrei una guida turistica di ... in inglese.
I'd like a book on ... with nice pictures.
Vorrei un libro su ... con belle illustrazioni.
I'd like an Italian/English dictionary.
Vorrei un dizionario italiano/inglese.
Do you keep books/newspapers/periodicals in English?
Avete libri/giornali in inglese?
Do you keep posters/theatre bills?
Avete poster/locandine?
Have you got a news-sheet of the entertainments on?
Avete un notiziario con il programma degli spettacoli?

240

STATIONERS AND ART SUPPLIES

biro	biro	'biro
brush	pennello	pen'nɛllo
canvas	tela	'tela
charcoal	carboncino	karbon'tʃino
crayon	matita	ma'tita
drawing pins	puntine	pun'tine
elastic bands	elastici	e'lastitʃi
envelopes	buste	'buste
exercise book	quaderno	kwa'dɛrno
with squared paper	a quadretti	akkwa'dretti
with lined paper	a righe	ar'rige
felt tipped pen	pennarello	penna'rɛllo
fountain pen	stilografica	stilo'grafika
glue	colla	'kɔlla
highlighter	evidenziatore	evidentsja'tore
Indian ink	china	'kina
ink	inchiostro	in'kjɔstro
labels	etichette	eti'kette
note pad	bloc notes	blɔk'nɔtes
notebook	taccuino	takku'ino
paints	colori	ko'lori
oil paints	a olio	a'ɔljo
tempera paints	a tempera	at'tɛmpera
acrylic paints	acrilici	a'krilitʃi
water colours	ad acquerello	adakkwe'rɛllo
paper	carta	'karta
carbon	carbone	kar'bone
wrapping	da imballo	daim'ballo
writing	da lettere	dal'lɛttere
gift wrapping	da regalo	darre'galo
pastels	pastelli	pas'tɛlli

pen	penna	'penna
pencil	lapis	'lapis
pencil leads	mine	'mine
pencil sharpener	temperamatite	tɛmperama'tite
postcard	cartolina	karto'lina
propelling pencil	portamine	pɔrta'mine
refill	ricambio	ri'kambjo
rubber	gomma	'gomma
ruler	righello	ri'gɛllo
set-square	squadra	'skwadra
sheets of drawing paper	fogli da disegno	'fɔʎʎi daddi'seɲɲo
sketch pad	album da disegno	'album daddi'seɲɲo
staple	graffetta	graf'fetta
string	spago	'spago
tube of paint	tubetto di colore	tu'betto diko'lore
typewriter ribbon	nastro per macchina da scrivere	'nastro per 'makkina das'krivere

LAUNDRY AND DRY CLEANERS

hand washing	lavaggio a mano	la'vaddʒo am'mano
dry cleaning	a secco	as'sekko
washing	ad acqua	a'dakkwa
launderette	lavanderia a gettone	lavande'ria addʒet'tone

I'd like to have this dress/suit dry cleaned.
Vorrei far lavare a secco questo vestito.

> **È necessario lavarlo ad acqua.**
> It will have to be washed.

I'd like to have this skirt pressed.
Vorrei far stirare questa gonna.

It's a/an ... stain.
È una macchia di ... .

> **Questa macchia è indelebile.**
> This stain won't come out.

It is a delicate garment.
È un capo delicato.

Do you do invisible mending?
Fate rammendi invisibili?

When will it be ready?
Per quando sarà pronto?

I need it before ... .
Mi occorre prima di ... .

This garment isn't mine.
Questo capo non è mio.

There's a hole here.
Qui c'è un buco.

5.4 SHOPPING

JEWELLERS

alabaster	alabastro	ala'bastro
amber	ambra	'ambra
amethyst	ametista	ame'tista
copper	rame	'rame
coral	corallo	ko'rallo
crystal	cristallo	kris'tallo
diamond	diamante	dia'mante
emerald	smeraldo	zme'raldo
enamel	smalto	'zmalto
glass	vetro	'vetro
gold	oro	'ɔro
ivory	avorio	a'vɔrjo
jade	giada	'dʒada
lacquer	lacca	'lakka
laminate	laminato	lami'nato
mother of pearl	madreperla	madre'pɛrla
onyx	onice	'ɔnitʃe
pearl	perla	'perla
plated	placcato	plak'kato
platinum	platino	'platino
quartz	quarzo	'kwartso
ruby	rubino	ru'bino
sapphire	zaffiro	dzaf'firo
semi-precious stone	pietra dura	'pjɛtra 'dura
silver	argento	ar'dʒɛnto
silver plate	argentato	ardʒen'tato
topaz	topazio	to'pattsjo
turquoise	turchese	tur'kese
white gold	oro bianco	'ɔro 'bjanko
strap	cinturino	tʃintu'rino
steel bracelet	di acciaio	diat'tʃajo
gold bracelet	d'oro	'dɔro

crocodile strap	di coccodrillo	*dikokko'drillo*
leather strap	di pelle	*di'pɛlle*
alarm clock	sveglia	*'zveʎʎa*
case	cassa	*'kassa*
chronometer	cronometro	*kro'nɔmetro*
dial	quadrante	*kwa'drante*
with calender day	con datario	*konda'tarjo*
with date	con calendario	*konkalen'darjo*
hand	lancetta	*lan'tʃetta*
movement	movimento	*movi'mento*
automatic	automatico	*auto'matiko*
quartz	al quarzo	*al'kwartso*
watch/clock	orologio	*oro'lɔdʒo*
wrist watch	da polso	*dap'polso*
pendulum clock	a pendolo	*ap'pɛndolo*
wall clock	da muro	*dam'muro*
winding	carica	*'karika*
bracelet	braccialetto	*brattʃa'letto*
brooch	spilla	*'spilla*
cameo	cammeo	*kam'mɛo*
chain	catena	*ka'tena*
cigarette case	portasigarette	*pɔrtasiga'rette*
cigarette lighter	accendino	*attʃen'dino*
cross	croce	*'krotʃe*
earrings	orecchini	*orek'kini*
jewellery case	astuccio	*as'tuttʃo*
medal	medaglia	*me'daʎʎa*
mounting	montatura	*monta'tura*
necklace	collana	*kol'lana*
pendant	pendente	*pen'dɛnte*
photograph frame	cornice	*kor'nitʃe*
ring	anello	*a'nɛllo*
setting	castone	*kas'tone*
tiepin	fermacravatta	*fermakra'vatta*
wedding ring	fede nuziale	*'fede nut'tsjale*

My watch has stopped. Can you repair it, please?
Mi si è fermato l'orologio. Può ripararlo?

I'd like to change the battery in my watch.
Vorrei cambiare la pila dell'orologio.

It gains/loses … minutes an hour.
Va avanti/indietro di … minuti ogni ora.

I'd like to change the strap/the glass.
Vorrei cambiare il cinturino/il vetro.

Can you repair the safety catch on this necklace?
Può riparare la sicura di questa collana?

It will be ready by … .
Sarà pronto per … .

I'd like to see a … watch, please.
Vorrei vedere un orologio …

    … subaqueous/stop- …
    … subacqueo/con cronometro.

    … good quality/cheap …
    … di marca/economico.

What stone/material is it?
Che pietra/materiale è?

Can I have another mounting on it?
Si può avere un'altra montatura?

Has it got a certificate of guarantee?
Ha il certificato di garanzia?

How much does this ring weigh?
Quanto pesa questo anello?

How many carats is it?
Di quanti carati è?

Are these cultivated pearls?
Queste perle sono coltivate?

Could you have them strung for me?
Può farmele infilare?

I'd like something less expensive.
Vorrei qualcosa di meno costoso.

PHOTOGRAPHY

aperture	diaframma	dja'framma
development	sviluppo	zvi'luppo
enlargement	ingrandimento	ingrandi'mento
exposure	esposizione	espozit'tsjone
filter	filtro	'filtro
focus	fuoco	'fwɔko
format	formato	for'mato
lens cover	tappo obbiettivo	'tappo obbjet'tivo
lens	obbiettivo	obbjet'tivo
light meter	esposimetro	espo'zimetro
movie-camera	cinepresa	tʃine'presa
negative	negativo	nega'tivo
overexposed	sovraesposto	sovraes'posto
photograph	fotografia	fotogra'fia
printing	stampa	'stampa
on … paper	su carta …	suk'karta
… glossy …	… lucida	'lutʃida
… matt	… opaca	o'paka
proofs	provini	pro'vini
release	scatto	'skatto
rewinding	riavvolgimento	riavvoldʒi'mento
self-timer	autoscatto	autos'katto
shot	inquadratura/	inkwadra'tura/
	posa	'pɔsa
shutter	otturatore	ottura'tore
telephoto lens	teleobbiettivo	teleobbjet'tivo
tripod	cavalletto	kaval'letto
underexposed	sottoesposto	sottoes'posto
view-finder	mirino	mi'rino
wide-angle	grandangolo	gran'dangolo

I'd like a … film for this camera, please.
Vorrei una pellicola … per questa macchina.

....

    ... black-and-white/colour ...
    ... in bianco e nero/ a colori ...
    ... 24/36 shot ...
    ... da 24/36 pose ...
    ... 100/200/400/1000 ASA ...
    ... da 100/200/400/1000 ASA ...
    ... ... DIN ...
    ... da ... DIN ...
    ... fine-grained/an artificial light type/daylight type ...
    ... a grana fine/per luce artificiale/normale ...

I'd like a cartridge/roll of film/diskette.
Vorrei un caricatore/un rullino/un dischetto.

This film has expired.
Questa pellicola è scaduta.

I'd like a ... minute cassette for this videocamera.
Vorrei una cassetta da ... minuti per questa videocamera.

I'd like to have this film/slide roll developed, please.
Vorrei sviluppare questo rullino/rullino di diapositive.

I'd like to have these negatives reprinted.
Vorrei ristampare questi negativi.

They will be ready for tomorrow.
Sono pronte per domani.

I'd like to see a(n) ... camera.
Vorrei vedere una macchina fotografica ...

    ... manual/automatic ...
    ... manuale/automatica.
    ... cheap/disposable ...
    ... a buon mercato/usa e getta.

Can you take the film out for me, please?
Mi può togliere il rullino?

Can you repair my camera?
Può riparare la mia macchina fotografica?

    Mi dovrà lasciare la macchina per qualche giorno.
    You will have to leave me the camera for a few days.

Non le conviene ripararla.
It's not worth repairing.

I'd like to have four passport photos done.
Vorrei fare quattro fototessera.

THE OPTICIAN

binoculars/ opera glasses	binocolo	bi'nɔkolo
contact lenses	lenti a contatto	'lɛnti akkon'tatto
soft	morbide	'mɔrbide
hard	rigide	'ridʒide
disposable	usa e getta	'uza ed'dʒɛtta
frame	montatura	monta'tura
magnifying glass	lente d'ingrandimento	'lɛnte dingrandi'mento

I'm looking for a pair of sunglasses.
Vorrei vedere un paio di occhiali da sole.

I'd like some reading glasses with 1 dioptrie lens.
Vorrei degli occhiali da lettura con lenti da 1 diottria.

I have broken my glasses. Can I get them repaired quickly?
Ho rotto gli occhiali, è possibile ripararli in poco tempo?

> **Sono pronti per domani.**
> They will be ready for tomorrow.

Could you loosen/tighten my frames, please?
Mi può allargare/restringere la montatura?

I'd like a soft (brand name) lens with ... graduation.
Vorrei una lente morbida [...] con ... gradazione.

I'd like some ... for contact lenses.
Vorrei ... per lenti a contatto.

    ... multi-use liquid ...
    ... del liquido multiuso ...

5.4 SHOPPING

... saline solution ...
... della soluzione salina ...

In Italy you can also buy stamps from the "Tabacchi" shops, but for these needs, see The Post, Area 3.3.

cigar	sigaro	'sigaro
cigarette-holder	bocchino	bok'kino
filter	filtro	'filtro
filter-tipped/	sigaretta con/	siga'retta kon/
-less cigarette	senza filtro	'sentsa 'filtro
lighter gas/petrol	gas/benzina	gas/ben'dzina
	per accendino	perattʃen'dino
papers	cartine	kar'tine
pipe cleaners	nettapipe	netta'pipe
pipe	pipa	'pipa
pipe scrape	scovolini	skovo'lini
tobacco	tabacco	ta'bakko
snuff	da fiuto	daf'fjuto
chewing	da masticare	dammasti'kare
pipe	da pipa	dap'pipa
cigarette	per sigarette	persiga'rette

I'd like ...
Vorrei ...

... a packet/a carton of ... .
... un pacchetto/una stecca di ... .

... some matches/a disposable lighter.
... dei fiammiferi/un accendino usa e getta.

... some cigars.
... dei sigari.

LOCAL HANDICRAFTS PRODUCTS

bisque	bisquit	*bis'kwi*
brass	ottone	*ot'tone*
copper	rame	*'rame*
damask	damaschino	*damas'kino*
earthenware	terracotta	*terra'kɔtta*
embroidery	ricami	*ri'kami*
folk posters/prints	stampe popolari	*'stampe popo'lari*
lace	pizzo	*'pittso*
majolica	maiolica	*ma'jɔlika*
ornament	soprammobile	*sopram'mɔbile*
papier maché	cartapesta	*karta'pesta*
pewter	peltro	*'peltro*
pillow-lace	tombolo	*'tombolo*
porcelain	porcellana	*portʃel'lana*
rug	tappeto	*tap'peto*
rush	giunco	*'dʒunko*
semi-precious stones	pietre dure	*'pjɛtre 'dure*
silk	seta	*'seta*
statuette	statuina	*statu'ina*
wicker	vimini	*'vimini*
wrought iron	ferro battuto	*'fɛrro bat'tuto*

What handicrafts/gastronomical products are typical?
Quali sono i prodotti artigianali/gastronomici tipici?

Is it handmade?
È fatto a mano?

5.4 SHOPPING

THE FLORIST

English	Italian	IPA
azalea	azalea	addza'lɛa
begonia	begonia	be'gɔnja
bulb	bulbo	'bulbo
camellia	camelia	ka'mɛlja
carnation	garofano	ga'rɔfano
chrysanthemum	crisantemo	krizan'tɛmo
cyclamen	ciclamino	tʃikla'mino
daffodil	narciso	nar'tʃizo
daisy	margherita	marge'rita
fuchsia	fucsia	'fuksja
gardenia	gardenia	gar'dɛnja
geranium	geranio	dʒe'ranjo
jasmine	gelsomino	dʒelso'mino
jonquil	giunchiglia	dʒun'kiʎʎa
lily	giglio	'dʒiʎʎo
mimosa	mimosa	mi'mosa
orchid	orchidea	orki'dɛa
plant	pianta	'pjanta
house plant	da appartamento	daapparta'mento
garden plant	da giardino	daddʒar'dino
succulent plant	grassa	'grassa
pot/vase	vaso	'vazo
rose	rosa	'rɔza
tulip	tulipano	tuli'pano
violet	viola	vi'ɔla

I'd like …
Vorrei …

    … a bunch of … .
    … un mazzo di … .
    … (some) fresh/wild flowers.
    … dei fiori freschi/di campo.

....

MAKING THE DECISION, NEGOTIATING, PAYING

How much does it cost?
Quanto costa?
Could you write down the price for me?
Può scrivermi il prezzo?
I don't want to spend more than … .
Non voglio spendere più di … .
Can you give me a discount?
Mi può fare un po' di sconto?

> **Spiacente, i prezzi sono fissi.**
> I'm sorry, but prices are fixed.
> **C'è uno sconto del 20%.**
> There is a 20% discount.
> **È già scontato.**
> It has already been discounted.
> **Sconto alla cassa.**
> Discount at the cashdesk.

Can I change it if necessary?
È possibile cambiarlo?

> **È possibile cambiare solo la taglia.**
> Only the size can be changed.
> **Se vuole cambiarlo, conservi lo scontrino.**
> If it has to be changed, keep the cash slip.
> **Gli articoli in liquidazione non si possono cambiare.**
> Articles in the sale cannot be changed.

■ **THE NEGATIVE DECISION**
It is too expensive.
È troppo caro.
No, it is not what I am looking for.
No, non è quello che cerco.
I will come back later.
Ripasso più tardi.

5.4 SHOPPING

■ THE POSITIVE DECISION

All right, I will take it.
Va bene, lo prendo.

Can you gift wrap it/make a packaging very secure, please?
Può fare un pacchetto regalo/una confezione robusta?

Can you have it delivered to my hotel/address, please?
Può farmelo avere in hotel/al mio recapito?

Can you forward it to me in Great Britain at this address?
Può spedirmelo in Gran Bretagna, a questo indirizzo?

> **Dovrò addebitarle … per le spese di spedizione.**
> I will have to charge you … forwarding expenses.
> **No, posso indicarle uno spedizioniere di fiducia.**
> No, but I can give you the name of a good forwarding agent.
> **Qualcos'altro?**
> Anything else?
> **Paghi alla cassa.**
> Please pay at the cash desk.

Where is the cash desk?
Dov'è la cassa?

Can I have a receipt/the invoice?
Posso avere la ricevuta/fattura?

Can I pay by cheque?
Posso pagare con un assegno?

> **Spiacente, non accettiamo assegni.**
> I am sorry. We don't accept cheques.

Can I pay by credit card/travellers' cheque?
Posso pagare con carta di credito, travellers' cheques?

Can I pay in British pounds?
Posso pagare in sterline?

> **Conservi lo scontrino.**
> Please keep the cash slip.

I'd like to change this article. Here is the cash slip.
Vorrei cambiare questo articolo, ecco lo scontrino.

Aeroplane 50
Airport 48-52
Animals 45
Anxiety 177
Automobile 147-155
Banks 131
Barber 140-142
Bed and Breakfast 94
Bills and Fees 98, 129-130, 180, 253-254
Boarding Houses 96
Bookshop 240
Breakfast 99
Bus 72-74
Calendar 19-20
Car Hire 78-81
Car Tow 60
Change 131
Cheeses 123
Chemist 185-188
Children 44, 137
Clothing 227-230
Coach 75-76
Coeliac disease 106
Colours 43
Commerce 221-224
Complaints 91-93, 127
Conversation 23-26, 190-193
Cosmetics 138
Customs 51-53
Damages 161
Danger 144-146
Date 18
Dentist 178
Directions 55, 163
Disabled 44
Documents 51, 77-78
Drinks 111
Electricity 238

Excursions 202-206
Eye glasses 180, 249
Fabrics 225
First Aid 181
First courses 116
Fish 121
Florist 252
Food stuffs 233
Fruit and Dessert 123-124
Games 218-220
Greetings 23, 192
Hairdresser 140-142
Handicrafts 251
Hi-Fi 239
Hotel 84-93
Hours 17
Household items 236
Hygiene 137
Illness 165-167
Jewelers 244
Kiosk 240
Laundry 243
Leather goods 230
Liquors 125
Lost and found 158
Meals 99, 113-126
Mechanic 58, 147-155
Medical Doctor 172-176
Monuments 194-201
Muggings 162
Museums 196-198
Navigation 64-65
Night clubs 211
Numbers 38-41
Optometrist 180, 249
Paper goods 241
Parking 59-60
Photography 247

Port 62
Post 132
Pots and Pans 236
Religion and Worship 142, 200
Reservations 85-87, 102, 209
Restaurants 101-105
Road accidents 155-157
Salads 115
Seeing a Doctor 172-184
Service station 57
Sewing 229
Shoes 230-232
Shows 207-211
Side dishes 117
Smokers 44
Snacks 126
Special Diets 106, 109
Sports 212-217
Station 66-69
Streets 54
Taxi 71
Telephones 89, 133-136
Temperature 22, 42
Theft 159
Tobacco 250
Traffic laws 55-57
Traffic violations 60-61
Train 69-70
Trauma 168
Undergarments 229
Underground 74
Utensils 236
Watches 245
Weather 21
Weights and Measures 41-42
Youth Hostels 96